MARY JEAN CHAN

Mary Jean Chan was born in Hong Kong in 1990. Chan is the author of the poetry collection *Flèche*, which was published in 2019. *Flèche* won the Costa Book Award for Poetry and was shortlisted for the International Dylan Thomas Prize, the John Pollard Foundation International Poetry Prize, the Jhalak Prize, the Seamus Heaney Centre First Collection Poetry Prize and a Lambda Literary Award. Their new book, *Bright Fear*, was shortlisted for the Forward Prize for Best Collection and the Writers' Prize. Chan served as a judge for the 2023 Booker Prize and is currently the 2023–4 Judith E. Wilson Poetry Fellow at the University of Cambridge.

ANDREW McMILLAN

Andrew McMillan was born in Barnsley in 1988. His debut collection of poetry, *physical*, was the only poetry book to ever win the *Guardian* First Book Award; it was also awarded a Somerset Maugham Award, an Eric Gregory Award, the Fenton Aldeburgh First Collection Prize and in 2019 was voted as one of the Top 25 Poetry Books of the Past 25 Years by the Booksellers Association. His second collection, *playtime*, won the inaugural Polari Prize, and a third collection, *pandemonium*, was published in 2021. He is Professor of Contemporary Writing at Manchester Metropolitan University and a fellow of the Royal Society of Literature. A debut novel, *Pity*, is out now.

100 QUEER POEMS

AN ANTHOLOGY BY

MARY JEAN CHAN
ANDREW McMILLAN

VINTAGE

3 5 7 9 10 8 6 4

Vintage is part of the Penguin Random House group of companies
whose addresses can be found at global.penguinrandomhouse.com

Penguin
Random House
UK

This edition published in 2024
First published in hardback by Vintage in 2022

penguin.co.uk/vintage

Typeset in 10.11/12.69pt Sabon LT Std by Jouve (UK), Milton Keynes
Printed and bound in Great Britain by Clays Ltd, Elcograf S.p.A.

The authorised representative in the EEA is Penguin Random House Ireland,
Morrison Chambers, 32 Nassau Street, Dublin D02 YH68

A CIP catalogue record for this book is available from the British Library

ISBN 9781529115338

Penguin Random House is committed to a sustainable future
for our business, our readers and our planet. This book is made
from Forest Stewardship Council® certified paper.

CONTENTS

Queer Childhoods, Queer Adolescence

Queer Domesticities

Queer Relationships

Queer Landscapes

vii

Queering the City

Queering Histories

Queer Futures

Some Statements, Some Questions

ANDREW McMILLAN

When I was sixteen I came out to my dad; that evening he knocked lightly on my bedroom door and, when I called out hello, stepped into the room and said, 'I think you should read this.' It was a copy of Thom Gunn's *Collected Poems*, red and thick as a slab of meat, Gunn's handsome face looking out from the cover. I fell in love. It wasn't that I saw myself in Gunn, or imagined living the life he did, it was that I saw for the first time that who I was might be worthy of poetry, worthy of literature.

*

The last time an anthology like this one came out from a trade press in the UK was almost four decades ago. Looking around at all the various poetries and range of voices we see being published now, and the twentieth-century voices they're in conversation with, I began to wonder what a new anthology might look like; how the tectonic plates of the page might have shifted in the intervening years.

*

Language is important to focus on, I know. The word 'queer' is still a contested space; for so long a slur, it has been reclaimed by large parts of the LGBTQ+ community, but still hurts some who remember the word hurled as a weapon towards them. For this anthology we contacted each (living) poet individually, where possible, to ensure they'd be happy being grouped under such a banner.

*

An anthology like this asks a necessary but difficult question: what is a queer poem? I wish I knew. The poems you're about to encounter are a hundred different ways we might arrive at an answer. Is a queer poem simply anything written by a poet who identifies themselves as queer? Is a queer poem one that is overtly queer in its subject matter? Is a queer poem one that queers the language, or the form, the very structure of what a poem is?

By including a poem in this anthology, are we shifting the way it, or its author, could be viewed? If some of these poems were included in an anthology of poems about mental health, or poems about freedom or loneliness, would that frame our reading of them? By looking at it through a queer lens, are we altering it? Is the version of the poem that exists in this anthology different from the one that existed before? This anthology is *100 Queer Poems*, not one hundred poems about queerness: what difference does that make?

*

And what of the poets? In amongst the newer names here are poets you may well be familiar with, they exist in the 'canon', that odd literary space which sometimes feels like an exclusive nightclub that has a dress-code nobody can describe, and a door policy that only exists through word-of-mouth. So often these are poets we know of *despite* their queerness, not because of it. Think of Langston Hughes, the poet of the Harlem Renaissance; think of John Ashbery of the New York School; think of Wilfred Owen, the war poet; think of W. H. Auden, the poet of a particular kind of Englishness. These are poets who often survive because there is another claim on their identity – they can neatly fit into another 'school', another 'movement' – and therefore are palatable for being taught in classrooms, for being read at weddings or funerals, for being remembered. What becomes of these poets if we centre that part of their identity that is often overlooked?

*

And what of the effect on you, the reader – why have you come here? Are you hoping for a glimpse into a life not your own (and isn't that perhaps what we ask of all literature?), or are you hoping to see something you might already have imagined? Perhaps you hope to use the poem almost as a window on a sunny day and see yourself refracted into the scene on the page. Perhaps you're looking for a sense of community. Perhaps you're striving towards a new language that might express who you are and how you can take yourself forward into the world. These are just some of the questions we were asking each other, and you might have better answers than us; more likely you have better questions you could ask.

*

This is an anthology that is arriving at a paradoxical time. The last half-decade has seen an explosion in new queer spaces for poetry: new magazines in which to publish; new and vital independent presses nurturing brilliant and disruptive talent; continued impetus from established publishers to celebrate and trust the work of queer poets; a new recognition and rediscovery of the queer poets of old. And yet what does this mean off the page, on the street, in day-to-day life? Hate crimes against queer people in the UK, for example, almost trebled in the five years that ended the 2010s (and these are just the incidents that were reported). There is a continuous, hideous and growing campaign of abuse and harassment towards the trans community, from politics, mainstream media and, sadly, within the queer community itself. Faced with this, what is it that poetry can do? On the one hand, nothing; and pretending poetry is the equivalent of legislative change and legal protection is false, and unhelpful. On the other hand, a community's collective imagination of itself – a reshaping and a remoulding of language, a subversion or altering of the everyday – might be how we begin to partly save ourselves.

*

At the turn of the millennium, when I was eleven or twelve, and the world and my body were turning into an unknown era, our school, like countless others, put together a time-capsule to bury, so future generations might remember the technologies and petty distractions of a bygone age. Anthologies are time-capsules too; if Mary Jean and I came back in ten years and did this project over again, things would already look very different.

*

So often in poetry, saying what something isn't can contain much more depth and weight than saying what something is. If I look out of the window and say, 'It's not raining', that's very different from saying, 'It's sunny.' In that spirit, here are a few things that this anthology isn't: it's not a generational anthology – there'll be time for that in the future and it's someone else's job. It's not an attempt at canon-building – it's just one more voice in an ongoing and flourishing conversation. It's not a destination, it's simply the next stage of the journey. Could that journey, at points, have reached different destinations? Almost always. An anthology, then, is simply an accumulation of the possible.

*

The only reason I write poetry is because I love to read it. Every time I turn a page of this anthology I'm sixteen again, back in my childhood bedroom, reading with excitement work that moved and inspired me. Maybe there's someone in your life who has just come out, maybe there's someone in your life who is struggling, maybe there's someone in your life for whom the language we currently have isn't adequate to describe who they are. Say you go and knock on their door, say you hand them a copy of this anthology. Say these poems put their arms around them, these poems open the curtains and point them towards places they haven't yet imagined. Say these poems give them pleasure. Say these poems give them hope. Say they find a piece of scrap paper and begin to write their own . . .

xiv

visibility

look at him   carrying flowers through the town
holding them tight in their plastic crinoline

who must he think he is   with those colours
the skimmed milk of the roses   the shy cheeks

of the tulips   moving like a silent
firecracker down the high street   it's as though

he wants us to look   to recall
all the bouquets we never took home

to our wives   and see now   how the wind
unfastens the ballgowns of the peonies

how their petals unfold and then fall
each one still whole and curling in the breeze

so now   with every step   a pink and falling lid
a trail of blinking eyes behind him

Finding Home in the Queer Poem

MARY JEAN CHAN

When Andrew invited me to co-edit this anthology of queer poetry, I remember feeling a rush of something akin to joy, gratitude and disbelief. Back when I was eighteen, I was closeted and depressed, as a first-year university student at business school in Hong Kong. I never anticipated that, a decade or so later, two important facets of my life – poetry and queerness – could come together so openly. Born and raised in Hong Kong during the 1990s and 2000s, I didn't know that queer writers existed, in either of the languages I spoke. I hadn't realised that some of the poets I had studied in my English literature classes were, in fact, queer: Elizabeth Bishop ('One Art'), W. H. Auden ('Funeral Blues') and Wilfred Owen ('Dulce et Decorum Est').

It seems difficult to imagine that 'homosexuality' was only officially declassified as a pathology or disease by the World Health Organization in 1990, the year I was born. During my teenage years, English literature provided an emotional safe space in which I could explore my emergent queer identity. It was while studying Shakespeare's *Twelfth Night* for the HKCEE (rough equivalent to GCSEs) that I experienced my first literary encounter with queerness, as I became fascinated by the character Viola/Cesario. After I transferred to the US to continue my undergraduate studies in 2009, I encountered poetry by Audre Lorde, June Jordan, Nikki Giovanni and many others. I participated in the 2012 College Unions Poetry Slam Invitational and was thrilled to watch poets such as Danez Smith take to the stage. That summer I graduated, came out to my parents and close friends, and fell deeply in love with poetry. I wrote a poem titled 'Birthday', about coming out at the age of twenty-one.

Arriving in England in the autumn of 2012, I remember meeting Jay Bernard (who kindly agreed to chat with me after we were introduced by a mutual friend) and being in awe of their work. My subsequent introduction to British queer poetry was marked by my belated encounter with the work of Carol Ann Duffy, Jackie Kay and others, including Caroline Bird's growing oeuvre, Andrew's *physical* in 2015 and Richard Scott's *Soho* in 2018. I was also reading American poets such as Natalie Diaz, Saeed Jones, Ocean Vuong, Chen Chen, Jericho Brown and Yanyi, many of whom have since had their books published in the UK. Without these trailblazers, I would not have dared to dream that my work might one day be published here too.

I am aware, however, that there are so many queer voices I have not encountered, partly for reasons Andrew and I have grappled with as we put this anthology together. In light of Section 28 – which was only repealed in 2000 in Scotland, and in 2003 in England and Wales – works by queer writers were actively shunned in classrooms. Yet others might not have felt safe to come out in their writing during this repressive time. Indeed, there is no reason a queer writer has to come out in their work; rather, it is the freedom to do so that matters. Writers who have migrated from countries that are less accepting of queer individuals (many of which are former British colonies) may also feel the need to protect themselves and their families by being less visible in queer spaces. A poet whom we'd invited declined to be included in our anthology precisely for this reason.

Taking these issues into consideration, we came up with a few parameters for this anthology: for it to contain poetry published in the UK by writers who have had at least a pamphlet or a full collection published; and to focus on poetry predominately from the twentieth century onwards, in order to attempt to reflect the multitude of queer, non-binary and trans voices that have emerged, particularly over the past few decades. Ultimately, we want to offer this anthology as a means of reclaiming those voices whose queerness has remained obfuscated throughout history, as well as bringing together and celebrating extraordinary contemporary voices whose writings have helped to define – and redefine – the meaning of queerness in our current time.

The poems we have chosen reflect our own proclivities, but we agreed as we selected them that each and every entry helps to expand upon the many definitions of what makes a poem 'queer'. According to Eric Keenaghan, 'to refer to a form of poetry as "queer", rather than as "LGBT", is to acknowledge how its authors challenge rigid and potentially divisive identity logics so as to forge new connections and alliances between communities and groups'. As someone who identifies as postcolonial, queer and Hong Kong-Chinese, I consider it reductive to view the concept of queerness as only applicable to one's sexuality, for to do so would be to ignore its nuances. The term queer could extend to issues such as race and racism, with Sara Ahmed observing how being racialised and othered is also an inherently queer experience. In their editorial to *Wasafiri*'s 'Queer Worlds/Global Queer' issue, Dean Atta and Andrew van der Vlies similarly define queer as that which '[plays] on its historical connotations of the counterproductive . . . the antisocial, [and] that which is in all ways aslant . . . to the normative'. In other words, to be queer is to refuse to follow certain straight lines.

As with all anthologies, ours cannot be comprehensive and will require refreshing as time goes on. Nonetheless, I was thrilled by the prospect of this anthology, because the thought of seeing it on a shelf in a bookstore deeply moved me. I remember walking into Gay's the Word in London for the first time in 2014 (after overcoming the usual fears of crossing that proverbial threshold) and thinking: I am safe here. Dear Reader, I hope this anthology does the same for you.

Answer

At the Poetry Café, some-
   one sipping tea once stared
      at me from across the room

and asked, are you a man or
   a woman? I want to know.
      I got up, moved my laptop,

book and coffee. I eventually
   replied, I would prefer not
      to answer that. Excuse me.

In deep autumn, on a busy
   London street, I want to
      summon myself to be free.

A Note on Reading

One of the great joys of reading an anthology is getting to choose how you want to move through it. You might open the book at a random page, take in whichever poem you are presented with and repeat this for days, weeks or months on end. You might go straight to the index, find the names of your favourite poets, then explore the poems that come before (and after) their work. These different ways of reading are valid and wonderful, but for those who require more structure, or who intend to move through this anthology from start to finish in a more methodical way, we have offered our take on how these poems might be grouped together.

We had in mind a movement from the internal to the external, from the self into the world, extending into questions about the future. Some categories are perhaps self-explanatory. 'Queer Childhoods, Queer Adolescence' looks at poems that bring language to those early moments in time, which seemed – perhaps for too long – beyond language: moments of queer self-discovery, instances of queer shame or the beginnings of queer attraction that took place during our teenage years. We then move into the home in 'Queer Domesticities', where we've gathered poets exploring the highs and lows inherent in our attempts at finding and creating safe spaces to dwell in with our chosen families.

We move further outwards into the physical and psychogeographical spaces that different writers have inhabited in 'Queer Landscapes' and in 'Queering the City'. 'Queering Histories' gathers poems that address marginalised histories, with poets exploring events ranging from the New Cross Fire to the aftermath of slavery in America. 'Queer Relationships' explores the threads and connections between individuals and communities, as well as within ourselves. Finally, 'Queer Futures' brings together poets whose writing speaks powerfully to the hopes, fears and dreams that we, as editors of this anthology, have for the future, as our societies continue to grapple with issues such as racism, climate disaster and transphobia.

Like all attempts at categorisation, ours is an artificial exercise; many of these poems could move into several sections at once to sit within intersecting Venn diagrams of language, emotion and thought. Think of our contents page as an initial attempt to offer a guide-map through these one hundred poems, the way the hosts of a party might seat certain people next to one another in the hope they'd particularly enjoy each other's company. If you'd rather curate your own guest list, or invite various poets out onto an imaginary balcony and spend all night talking among yourselves, please do. Whether you start your reading journey here or further along in the anthology, we hope you will find what you are looking for.

Mary Jean Chan & Andrew McMillan

QUEER CHILDHOODS, QUEER ADOLESCENCE

COLETTE BRYCE

A Spider

I trapped a spider in a glass,
a fine-blown wineglass.
It shut around him, silently.
He stood still, a small wheel
of intricate suspension, cap
at the hub of his eight spokes,
inked eyes on stalks; alert,
sensing a difference.
I meant to let him go
but still he taps against the glass
all Marcel Marceau
in *the wall that is there but not there*,
a circumstance I know.

JEN CAMPBELL

The Bear

I sit in the dark in a blue jumper that scratches and ask you
how you would draw a bear if you'd never seen one before.

You don't seem to understand the question.

It's a very important question, I say.

It's a stupid question, you say. I know what bears look like. I'll
draw one for you now.

The paper is too dark to see.

I steal your pencil and persist that you have never seen a bear
in the flesh and photographs are all well and good but you
have never touched a bear or hidden from a bear or felt the
breath of a bear on your very human skin.

Also, how do you know I am not a bear? I ask.

Because you're not, you say. Go to sleep.

I bristle under the duvet, my hot lungs Ursa Major.

ELIZABETH BISHOP

Sestina

September rain falls on the house.
In the failing light, the old grandmother
sits in the kitchen with the child
beside the Little Marvel Stove,
reading the jokes from the almanac,
laughing and talking to hide her tears.

She thinks that her equinoctial tears
and the rain that beats on the roof of the house
were both foretold by the almanac,
but only known to a grandmother.
The iron kettle sings on the stove.
She cuts some bread and says to the child,

It's time for tea now; but the child
is watching the teakettle's small hard tears
dance like mad on the hot black stove,
the way the rain must dance on the house.
Tidying up, the old grandmother
hangs up the clever almanac

on its string. Birdlike, the almanac
hovers half open above the child,
hovers above the old grandmother
and her teacup full of dark brown tears.
She shivers and says she thinks the house
feels chilly, and puts more wood in the stove.

It was to be, says the Marvel Stove.
I know what I know, says the almanac.
With crayons the child draws a rigid house
and a winding pathway. Then the child
puts in a man with buttons like tears
and shows it proudly to the grandmother.

But secretly, while the grandmother
busies herself about the stove,
the little moons fall down like tears
from between the pages of the almanac
into the flower bed the child
has carefully placed in the front of the house.

Time to plant tears, says the almanac.
The grandmother sings to the marvelous stove
and the child draws another inscrutable house.

EMILY HASLER

What Gretel Knows

Gretel knows what to say to the boy who thinks we're saved.
Gretel knows, put a girl in water and she'll drown; boil it,
she'll cook. Gretel knows there's no salvation; only storage,
refrigeration, freezing. A fairytale of Tupperware, stained
and scratched, sudded beside the sink. Even old crones
have to eat. We be fat. We be lean. Gretel knows it's just
a change of state, conduction of heat. Gretel knows
how we swell and settle like dough with weight of air, time.
The child hacked from the wolf's stomach, pulled from the
    womb,
taken from the oven or the pot. But Gretel knows it is too late.
The ingredients in us activate. A raising. Our edges puff and blur,
give and take of the world about us. It doesn't matter, Gretel
    told him,
she knows that the house is cake for fuck's sake. The earth
is seasoning. Our sweet flesh is so tender it flakes between
our fingers. Gretel knows. That the wicked stepmother,
the old crone, Baba Yaga, me—Gretel—we are all the same.
Archetypal and obsessed with our stomachs. Gretel says:
This is the bread that broke the body. This is my body: take it.
    Eat.
This is the tongue that licked the bowl of the cement mixer
    clean.

ALICE HILLER

valentine

a china heart
enamelled with violets

lies in a leather box
lined with silk

the heart shuts
with a golden clasp

on a doily
these words

*I once belonged
to someone dear*

note: this memory comes shagged with flies

MATTHEW HAIGH

Vintage Barbie Chest of Drawers

What I love about videogames with poor graphics is the bitty-ness of them.

I like reality rendered through a diorama, a plywood façade, the dryly domestic reflected in pink plastic.

This is why I preferred playing with Barbie as a boy – her assortment of accessories in miniature: PVC handbags, clamshell compacts, sun hats & cycling helmets.

My grandparents thought it meant I would *turn out funny*.

But it's difficult for a 6 year old to articulate how few things are as satisfying as the click of a tiny drawer in a tiny cabinet.

JAY GAO

Persons Not Welcome

I left all my slippery toy soldiers on the washing machine lid
    those wet miniatures
        travel sized men I will have to scoop up in the morning

I clutched my dirty clothes to my chest like a bouquet of limbs
in last night's dream
    I was a child   lost in that hallway again
I was a newly sewn doll longing to be filled up with sand

on a branch I saw three apples   made of metal
    waiting to mutate

a bruise the size of an eye leading to
                    rust the size of my nation

KOSTYA TSOLAKIS

totality

solar eclipse, Crete, 11 August 1999

the car's an incubator/ even
with the windows down/ squashed
in the back of the boxy rental/ I'm taller
than both my parents/ radio says/ today
will hit 40°C/ we're too far south/ to wow
at the diamond ring/ for the sky to dim/
pacing the water's edge/ in the brooding
heat/ the clammy nylon of my swim shorts
clings/ I kick and kick/ the breathless
sea/ next month/ I can learn to drive/ buy
alcohol/ gamble/ next month/ I'll find
my cool release/ in the shadows
of England's parks/ next month/
next month/

PETER SCALPELLO

ode to tracksuit

my hungered polyester   thighs show you no
         mercy   if you can even fathom
      my shape through all   this rustle

            what happened to
            your levi's, dude

         remember when we used
      to sport these bottoms   as a uniform
         as   armour against ridicule

         we grew out of this   didn't we
remember when   we donned matching shell suits
      & drank   cider from three-litre containers
      that served us almost everything   we needed
               to be able to swallow
our attractions & get with   the girls by the river
         between dregs forming   fag holes

               i know you
      remember when we ruined   our friendship
            by circling the inside of each
      other's cheeks with   underdeveloped tongues

            the rub of that nothing
      fabric was like   touching skin & my
         crotch in activewear could keep
               nothing secret

now you   jog up to me in dalston
with the same leaden legs
that fled from teenage   shame panting
for what i guess is   reclamation or subversion or
both things   but in the form
of an easily removable manliness

remember when we donned
matching shell suits &   were happy
to be invisible

take off   your trackies & show
me what hasn't
changed underneath

13

TROY CABIDA

Buddy

He moulds a hand into my right shoulder
to soften the nervous muscle,

the friction between open mouth and stubbled cheek
revealing the truth in how much I've learnt

to find pleasure in the things that fight back.
I explore his tall, his swimmer lean,

enjoy touch as in gentle not penetrating,
let my body be a Friday afternoon.

In between exhales he calls me
stupid names like bro or buddy

as part of the experiment,
to be a sounding board of sorts,

to help make peace with old faces
who couldn't possibly give back.

HOLLY PESTER

Villette

In the novel Villette, either I or Lucy Snowe live and work in a girls' school that either she or I found in a small French town. She has nowhere / I have nowhere and no thing in which to hide any of her few / my few possessions. Her mattresses / my mattresses and bedding in the dormitory where she sleeps / I sleep are checked over daily, and she suspects / I suspect that her / my desk in the classroom is also looked through.

She has nowhere / I have nowhere to hide a letter that was sent to her / to me by Dr Graham, who she has a heavy and imaginative crush on / who I have a heavy and imaginative crush on.

She invests / I invest in the letter a devotional adoration that mismatches the friendly goodwill it was written with.

I / Lucy guess that the schoolmistress has snatched, read and then returned the letter to under her / my bed. Lucy panics over her / my lack of private space and makes the eccentric decision to bury the letter in the garden grounds of the school.

She folds the pages tightly / I fold the pages tightly, wrap them in a silk handkerchief dipped in oil, curl them into a glass bottle and hermetically seal the bottle with wax.

She buries the bottle / I bury the bottle under the roots of an ivy bush in an area of the garden that is haunted by either me or the ghost of a nun who was buried alive.

In this gesture / in my gesture, Lucy Snowe rejects the possibility of possessing the letter. She applies / I apply a fantastical value to the letter. The letter passes into an earthed state of absence. I use / Lucy uses burial as a way to disown the letter and to refuse being privately subjected by the letter. She instead / I instead ecstatically ritualise her poverty / my poverty, and her otherness / my otherness to ownership of objects, and evacuate the self into love.

NATHAN WALKER

Carrying in the Mouth
Excerpts

I

Too recently for my liking I went to speak but could not. I was invited to speak an answer that would also be a disclosure, and despite us both already knowing what the unsaid sentence was, it still needed to be voiced aloud. This would *do* something—as voices can but are rarely given credit for doing.

Speaking is a rising, dynamic opening and creation of an event. Forming undisclosed things into vocal sound is difficult because these things often have a weight and a heat that more casual forms of speech don't have. These are sounds that have already been shaped internally by our gut and by bursas, tissue, muscles, cells—impressed by the shapes between the organs and pressed by memories held at locations in the torso, the thigh and the nape. An embodied vocality, these are events of the body, the body in our mouths. Sometimes there are things you cannot bear to speak.

Yet, the event of speaking a disclosure is not only about speaking, it is also about hearing your own voice sound this thing aloud. The fact of the voice. It leaves your lips and touches your ears and in that movement between the lip and the ear it holds your face / holds you.

In this instance, when I was invited to speak, I engaged my vocal chords, I pushed my breath against my sternum in anticipation and readiness, and as I was already internally, repeatedly saying the saying, despite my trying to release it, I remained utterly silent—wordlessness—the sound I made before this suspension was a half heave. I had attempted to throw my words out, to release them, expecting them to emerge fully and intact, but something held the sound back and I sat in silence. I was frozen for minutes, my mouth parted ready to speak but not truly ready to hear myself say. I didn't manage it, I gave in, sometimes there are things you cannot bear to hear.

4

When I came out to my parents at seventeen, I had the word 'sorry' running parallel to all my rehearsed sentences but was determined not to say it. In the heat of the saying that I was gay, and the rushed fighting of emotional response—knowing that my twin brother was in the other room 'just in case', as he said to me, 'anything kicks off'—my fingers folded back over my cuffs blotting my eyes with my sleeve, I was determined to not apologise.

I got caught out by my own rule almost immediately. In defence to the first responses from my parents I said I'm sorry if, and trailing off I corrected myself, no I'm not sorry, I'm not.

I'm not. I am. I declare. I use these words. I own them, I hold them. I carried this particular unsaid sentence with me, we carry them in our mouths. Grafted to our gums, unable to swallow. Years later I carry other sentences, so much longer than three words, coiled around my mouth several times in order to keep them.

Carrying in the mouth does two things. Firstly, it threatens to reveal itself, and you, by slipping out in various ways. This may be all of a sudden or slowly inching out or even attaching itself to other sounds, words and sighs. It is never not present in all other spoke words and sounds, everything else passes through that which is carried in the mouth. And because of this, carrying in the mouth does a second thing, it alters the sound of our voice. It unfolds as a tone gathered through our speech and others can hear this.

In many ways the things we carry in our mouths may be heard more than we like to admit. The sound of my voice exposed me so many times in adolescence, it could reveal me with only a single syllable or even a cough or ahem. The voice is a revelation; it has the ability to lay bare. Queer voices cut through unsafe spaces in curves. Queer voices spiral and raise with the heat of the breath carried up from the knees. Queer voices hold you.

If we cannot bring ourselves to speak then the things we carry can be practiced, or mouthed, or even spoken to oneself but this is different to hearing your own voice in the presence of others. There are many mouths inside your mouth, and they extend with and extend as sound, as tone, as stolon.

5

Planished, his voice produces a climate. I like to call the throat the marshes and hold them in the palm of my hand, cambered like the hull of a ship. Everyone knows bloods taste. Saying is a ligature a cupping the ears. Flushed as in flat, it binds me to the action, it does not loosen. The body is pressed, to the roof, until it feels nothing like a body. I am really trying to give light to a low planted seed, simply by opening my mouth. Pierced the guts. The climber, teacher, audio, discipline. Beneath a room with (loud) speakers coiled inside and my head is tilted back—vocal—but sourced from the underside of my chin. A quiet sound, scratches down to the waist until it feels like not having a body. Dry and wet.

Once I put my baby teeth, collected by my mam and given to me as a gift, I put them back, back into my adult mouth. The past and the present created an event, a gathering, an action. The impression of carrying in the mouth, something you can't say and can't put back.

KARL KNIGHTS

First Meeting

I'd never met another autistic person.
My SENCO wanted me to tutor him.
I was fifteen, he was twelve. I waited for him
in the room we'd been assigned. I could hear
the other SEN kids, laughing and screaming, arguing
with their TAs. Then he came in, Tom. He sat down.
My stims – tapping my teeth,
twiddling my fingers, spinning my keys –
were exactly mirrored. He stared at the floor
as I used to. He fidgeted, bounced,
rocked. He told me he didn't understand
why the girl next to him in Maths
keeps passing notes and smiling?
Why do teachers insist on eye contact
when it means nothing?
I said I didn't know either.
Try and look at their noses, or their foreheads.
I pulled out some of the board games left in our room,
not Monopoly – we sussed we couldn't do numbers.
When the bell rang neither of us knew how to leave.

QUEER DOMESTICITIES

CHEN CHEN

I Invite My Parents to a Dinner Party

In the invitation, I tell them for the seventeenth time
(the fourth in writing), that I am gay.

In the invitation, I include a picture of my boyfriend
& write, *You've met him two times. But this time,*

*you will ask him things other than can you pass the
whatever. You will ask him*

*about him. You will enjoy dinner. You will be
enjoyable. Please RSVP.*

They RSVP. They come.
They sit at the table & ask my boyfriend

the first of the conversation starters I slip them
upon arrival: *How is work going?*

I'm like the kid in *Home Alone*, orchestrating
every movement of a proper family, as if a pair

of scary yet deeply incompetent burglars
is watching from the outside.

My boyfriend responds in his chipper way.
I pass my father a bowl of fish ball soup—*So comforting,*

isn't it? My mother smiles her best
Sitting with Her Son's Boyfriend

Who Is a Boy Smile. I smile my Hurray for Doing
a Little Better Smile.

Everyone eats soup.
Then, my mother turns

to me, whispers in Mandarin, *Is he coming with you
for Thanksgiving? My good friend is & she wouldn't like*

this. I'm like the kid in *Home Alone*, pulling
on the string that makes my cardboard mother

more motherly, except she is
not cardboard, she is

already, exceedingly my mother. Waiting
for my answer.

While my father opens up
a *Boston Globe*, when the invitation

clearly stated: *No security
blankets.* I'm like the kid

in *Home Alone*, except the home
is my apartment, & I'm much older, & not alone,

& not the one who needs
to learn, has to—*Remind me*

what's in that recipe again, my boyfriend says
to my mother, as though they have always, easily

talked. As though no one has told him
many times, what a nonlinear slapstick meets

slasher flick meets psychological
pit he is now co-starring in.

Remind me, he says
to our family.

LEO BOIX

Oval Table
from *Table Variations*

Profane
four-legged thing
a holy place of gatherings
father mother three kids a ghost
eating asado Sunday mass barbecue
sins familiar sins scattered all over
the old checkered tablecloth Pray
one day you'll have a family like this
all these traditions will pass on
to you *Pray!* this broken table
now dies slowly now lies
alone in a toolshed
somewhere
South.

DEAN ATTA

Strawberry Thief

William Morris curtains
surround the dining table
nested in the bay window.
These thrushes never able
to reach the strawberries.

Maybe they're waiting
for someone to wish them
bon appetit, as we do
with each other. Neither of us
French, but we don't say
the equivalent in Greek,
Jamaican patois or Italian.

We're two Englishmen
in Scotland. Tonight we eat
Shepherd's Pie. You've made it
for me for the first time.
It's my comfort food,
reminds me of home-home,

my mother's home
in London, where we call
the living room the 'sala'
even though the Greek is 'salóni' –
village Greek, she tells me.

She is alone in her sala.
Her daughter and granddaughters
nearby, but unable to visit.

Me, here, in Glasgow.
The rest of her family
in Cyprus and Switzerland.

You don't miss your family,
you admit to me.
Your Shepherd's Pie
is better than my mother's,
I admit to you.

GREGORY WOODS

That Sweet

We're eating messages,
chewing on the gristle of
the hard to say, the sharp-edged bone
of what-I-want-to-tell-you-but-
don't-dare. Munch. Crunch. Lunch.
There's rhyme at least,
if not a lot of reason.
I'm reading a whole new course into
each of your expressions –
we ought to have another wine
for each, perhaps a simple
sorbet too to emphasise
a new direction. Munch!
Crunch! Lunch! Music to my
intestines. And think of this:
with fare like this
there's never any question of
an end to hunger.
I'm famished for another word from you,
another phrase, a joke,
a nothing sweet as, well,
as sweet as the adjective itself.
As sweet as that. That sweet!

COLIN HERD

Hint hint

Sweet pea you are filthy
the same tea towel for
plates and pots
just leave it and I'll sort it later
I like to move them around on a tray
4 in a bed's on and somebody just licked
the sink
Don't get me started on your armpits
or forever hold your tongue
I'm no parsleyphobe
your knuckles are pink dolphins
chomping through that water
but sweet pea you are filthy
there's nowhere this poem can go
I'll dry; you wash
I don't mean the dishes

RICHARD SCOTT

love version of
from *after Verlaine*

tonight I watched you sleep
naked on the futon
face down sweaty like a small child
and knew that everything else was bullshit

it's so hard to stay alive these days
or sane
so keep on snoring danny
while I guard you like a rottweiler

being in love with you is fucking awful
cause one day you'll stop breathing
in this grey light you already look dead

but then you smile thank fuck
what are you dreaming about baby wake up
tell me if the word soul still means anything

PADRAIG REGAN

Aubade with Half a Lemon on the Summer Solstice

Sleep was a paltry wafer
after we'd come back
from watching the tide
expose the beach's softer
districts & the sun
beginning to spill through
a murder-hole in an
architrave of clouds. The
open half of a lemon had
been left in the kitchen,
weeping into the grain of
the table. The table
corresponds with the
woody pips; the lemon
corresponds with a
breakfast of fried eggs &
butter melting into a slice
of toast. It donated its
other half to the piquancy
of gin & tonics. I squeeze
out what's left of the juice
& a paper cut I didn't
know I had begins to sing
Puccini's Vissi d'Arte.

The Whistler

All of a sudden she began to whistle. By all of a sudden
I mean that for more than thirty years she had not
whistled. It was thrilling. At first I wondered, who was
in the house, what stranger? I was upstairs reading, and
she was downstairs. As from the throat of a wild and
cheerful bird, not caught but visiting, the sounds war-
bled and slid and doubled back and larked and soared.

Finally I said, Is that you? Is that you whistling? Yes, she
said. I used to whistle, a long time ago. Now I see I can
still whistle. And cadence after cadence she strolled
through the house, whistling.

I know her so well, I think. I thought. Elbow and ankle.
Mood and desire. Anguish and frolic. Anger too.
And the devotions. And for all that, do we even begin
to know each other? Who is this I've been living with
for thirty years?

This clear, dark, lovely whistler?

RACHEL MANN

St Elisabeth Zacharias

Come. Beyond thirst, beyond tending,
Where rose petals crisp, water greens
In a vase.

Move closer. Breathe my dust, my very flesh
Settling. Be dust with me. Here where
We place the things we've gathered -

The china labradors,
The endless cats,
The *Cliff Richard* plates.

Isn't this how it should be? Piling
Fold on fold, letting gravity pull
On our bones, till we can resist no more?

Don't touch me. My cells ache. My skin
So thin spiders fall through.
It would be a sin to hold someone else.

NANCY CAMPBELL

Sleepers

I write these words at night in a small room with your fountain
pen / *scratch scratch* the split nib across the page and I / pause
for a word and remember another room / a different quiet
waiting for a word / a time before and after speech: / I lie in
bed, while curving rails below pull / a tram through silence
into sudden sound / the wheels scrape / an edge of metal
grating on another edge / a screech repeating through the
dawn until you wake / a sound that won't unspool into the
distance where the rails are straight / only at this turn will
the journey reach a sleeper's mind –

How could I see so clearly / the tram weigh down the track
with its steel haste / lying in darkness on those sheets, my
warm skin against yours? / How did I know your cool skin
without seeing it – and the only other warmth your breath? /
And there was silence, and another tram, and more silence
which I could not measure / then rush of water in pipes, the
murmur of morning. How can I hear it now / one thousand
miles, hundreds of days away? / Your breath, ribs rising under
your cool skin, my hand on your heart. / Your heart, unseen,
working those hours in silence / silence, no need for a word. //

JEE LEONG KOH

In His Other House

> *In this house there is no need to wait for the verdict of history*
> *And each page lies open to the version of every other.*
> — Eiléan Ní Chuilleanáin, 'In Her Other House'

In my other house too, books fill the floor-to-ceiling shelves,
not only books on stock markets, seven habits, ghost stories,
but also poetry, Arthur Yap, Cyril Wong, Alfian Sa'at,
and one who moved away and who wrote Days of No Name.

My father comes home from the power station. When rested
(and this is how I know this is not real) he reads to us again,
for the seventh time, Philip Jeyaretnam's Abraham's Promise
in a quiet voice, unbroken by a frightened young supervisor.

When he closes the book, my dead grandfather stirs heavily
and says a word or two, that really says he has been listening.
And my beloved, knowing his cue, jumps up from the couch
to clear the dishes, for, he says, dishes don't wash themselves.

Softly brightened by a feeling I do not hurry to identify,
I move to the back of him and put my arms around his waist.
His muscles twitch like the needle on a motorboat's dashboard
as he turns a bone china plate against a rough cotton cloth.

The light from the window looks like a huge, blank sea.
In this other house there will be time to fill it but right now
the bell intones in silver, and here, on a surprise night visit,
are my sister and her two daughters coming through the door.

GAIL McCONNELL

Untitled/Villanelle

I have often longed to see my mother in the doorway.
> – Grace Paley

Because having a father made me want a father.
> – Sandra Newman

I have often longed to see my mother
tap-dance in a top hat like she did before he died –
having (had) a father made me want a father.

A mather / madder / mether is a measure
that keeps its shape & holds what's stored inside –
I   often   . see my mother.

Mistype the word it stretches to a fother
(a cartload carries fodder, hitched outside) –
           a father made me.

You come to know the one against the other.
You measure till the meanings coincide.
I have often longed to see my father.

My mother's mother died before her daughter was a mother.
Alone, she gave me all she could provide –
(not) having a father made me want (to be) a father.

What am I to you? Mother? Father? Neither?
Like cells, names split & double, unified.
I have often longed to   mother
mother father fother mather matherfother fothermather

37

ERICA GILLINGHAM

Let's Make a Baby with Science

We can't fuck our way to a family
so let's do the furthest thing possible
from the intimacy of our bedroom.

Let's invite a dozen medical professionals
to ask us invasive questions with varying
degrees of empathy & bedside manner.

Let's test my veins, my blood, my uterus,
my textbook ovaries until we lose track
of our week-on-week appointments.

Let's find ourselves speechless after each shot,
not knowing how to respond to each other,
syringes empty, sharp's box lying at our feet.

Let's turn down invitations to all-night discos,
weekend benders, & sweaty basement raves
because we've got at-home stimulants to do.

Let's call the process a cycle, as if it's natural,
then spend two weeks worrying about having
enough piss in my bladder for the pregnancy test.

And when it doesn't work, think it should work,
we won't know why, may never know why,
then we'll do it all over again.

And again.

And again.

And again.

AARON KENT

Small, Wingless

I was born on a two piece
pay later, an interest
rate dictated by my
birth centile. I was breeched
in instalments, spread
across the year; my mother

birthed an overdraft limit,
christened the mass in
common tongue. Learnt
to make space a premium,
notched into the damp
like a silverfish pedalling

into the core of us. My
mother's loss in the plaster-
board shaped like every
pet we begged to need
us. My father counting
grief in a shell in the roof,

            the difference between
            me and a mortgage
            is that gutting a house
            takes time.

JOHN ASHBERY

They Dream Only of America

They dream only of America
To be lost among the thirteen million pillars of grass:
"This honey is delicious
Though it burns the throat."

And hiding from darkness in barns
They can be grownups now
And the murderer's ashtray is more easily --
The lake a lilac cube.

He holds a key in his right hand.
"Please," he asked willingly.
He is thirty years old.
That was before

We could drive hundreds of miles
At night through dandelions.
When his headache grew worse we
Stopped at a wire filling station.

Now he cared only about signs.
Was the cigar a sign?
And what about the key?
He went slowly into the bedroom.

"I would not have broken my leg if I had not fallen
Against the living room table. What is it to be back
Beside the bed? There is nothing to do
For our liberation, except wait in the horror of it.

And I am lost without you."

J. T. WELSCH

The Man from the Phone Company

A man from the phone company
hoists his great blue handset,
settling on the savage rhythms
it will accentuate for him.

I watch because I cannot listen.
In town, you're buying something
you found last week, not hidden
in the library, as I've told him.

While he works, I see your paper-
white, down-pencilled belly until
another stone-eyed blackbird
has a go at our leafless grapes,

nearly as dark as it by now.
The man has taken no notice.
My heart goes out to hands like
his, like paws. I need their pity.

Spent

Late August morning I go out to cut
spent and faded hydrangeas—washed
greens, russets, troubled little auras

of sky as if these were the very silks
of Versailles, mottled by rain and ruin
then half-restored, after all this time . . .

When I come back with my handful
I realize I've accidentally locked the door,
and can't get back into the house.

The dining room window's easiest;
crawl through beauty bush and spirea,
push aside some errant maples, take down

the wood-framed screen, hoist myself up.
But how, exactly, to clamber across the sill
and the radiator down to the tile?

I try bending one leg in, but I don't fold
readily; I push myself up so that my waist
rests against the sill, and lean forward,

place my hands on the floor and begin to slide
down into the room, which makes me think
this was what it was like to be born:

awkward, too big for the passageway . . .
Negotiate, submit?
                        When I give myself
to gravity there I am, inside, no harm,

the dazzling splotchy flowerheads
scattered around me on the floor.
Will leaving the world be the same

—uncertainty as to how to proceed,
some discomfort, and suddenly you're
—where? I am so involved with this idea

I forget to unlock the door,
so when I go to fetch the mail, I'm locked out
again. Am I at home in this house,

would I prefer to be out here,
where I could be almost anyone?
This time it's simpler: the window-frame,

the radiator, my descent. Born twice
in one day!
              In their silvered jug,
these bruise-blessed flowers:

how hard I had to work to bring them
into this room. When I say *spent*,
I don't mean they have no further coin.

If there are lives to come, I think
they might be a little easier than this one.

QUEER RELATIONSHIPS

PATIENCE AGBABI

Josephine Baker Finds Herself

She picked me up
like a slow-burning fuse. I was down
that girls' club used to run in Brixton,
on acid for fuel. Lipstick lesbians,
techno so hardcore it's spewing out Audis.
She samples my heartbeat and mixes it with
vodka on the rocks. I'm her light-skinned, negative,
twenty-something, short black wavy-bobbed diva.
She purrs *La Garçonne, fancy a drink?* I say
Yes. She's crossing the Star Bar like it's a catwalk. So sleek!
A string of pearls, her flapper dress
studded with low-cut diamonds
through my skin, straight to my heart.
Twenties chic! She works
me up and down. I worship
the way she looks.

The way she looks
me up and down. I worship
twenties chic. She works
through my skin, straight to my heart
studded with low-cut diamonds.
A string of pearls her flapper dress.
Yes! She's crossing the Star Bar like it's a catwalk so sleek
she purrs, la garçonne! *Fancy a drink?* I say.
Twenty-something, short, Black, wavy-bobbed diva:
Vodka on the rocks, I'm her light-skinned negative.
She samples my heartbeat and mixes it with
techno so hardcore it's spewing out Audis

on acid for fuel. *Lipstick Lesbians*,
that girls' club used to run in Brixton
like a slow-burning fuse. I was down.
She picked me up.

KAE TEMPEST

We bought new sheets

I am telling a story, enjoying myself
I know because my hand is conducting
my descriptions
We are driving through golden light
And your body is inclining towards me
at all points
As it does when you're happy with me

The lake shines on the watery sun,
the dog sleeps on the bank, one eye
watching
as we clutch each other's bodies beneath
the darkening mountain
and close our eyes underwater

Night buzzes around us

we shake it till it billows then snap it
tight,
pull its edges and fold it under
like a pair of real adults

MARINA TSVETAEVA

from *Girlfriend*

12

Moscow's hills are blue, the warm air
   tasting of dust and tar.
I sleep all day or else I laugh
   as if well again after winter.

I go home quietly without regretting
   the poems I haven't written,
the sound of wheels, or roasted almonds
   matter more than a quatrain.

My head is magnificently empty,
   my heart dangerously full;
my days are like tiny waves
   seen from a small bridge.

Perhaps my look is too tender
   for air that is barely warm.
I am already sick of summer –
   though hardly recovered from winter.

13 March 1915

Translated by David McDuff

W. H. AUDEN

Funeral Blues

Stop all the clocks, cut off the telephone,
Prevent the dog from barking with a juicy bone,
Silence the pianos and with muffled drum
Bring out the coffin, let the mourners come.

Let aeroplanes circle moaning overhead
Scribbling on the sky the message 'He is Dead'.
Put crêpe bows round the white necks of the public doves,
Let the traffic policemen wear black cotton gloves.

He was my North, my South, my East and West,
My working week and my Sunday rest,
My noon, my midnight, my talk, my song;
I thought that love would last forever: I was wrong.

The stars are not wanted now; put out every one,
Pack up the moon and dismantle the sun,
Pour away the ocean and sweep up the wood;
For nothing now can ever come to any good.

KAZIM ALI

Wrong Star

Wrong star I chose
To sail under alone
I did not want
To be alone
Brought or abandoned
Those nights when
I did not know
Who could know
Am I invited
Do you remember
Which question
Needs answer

JOSHUA JONES

On Accuracy

Isn't it the law that no fuck off, I thread
My gender thru a horseshoe to stomp
Your face. The point is to make the point

Sharp enough to cut, to sculpt a future
More liveable, to this extent love is a weapon
Carved on ambivalence, soaking up poison

& cure. The point is also to miss
The point, we are not weapon but flesh
We are circumscribed & sore, we have cried

We're alive. The aspiration of breathing to drape
Its wreckage across the wound, to see
The wound as not your own but the wreckage

Precisely. Some days it is enough to walk
Down the street to the sea without drowning
The waves out slowly encroach

Horizon insufflated by falling, I meet
Lovers, continents & islands. It's not
That I don't love you endlessly, rattled

On the carapace, giddily small, but the effort
So much simply to not be undone, the zip
Of our life, shall we meet for breakfast?

MARTHA SPRACKLAND

Go Away and Then Come Back

When I creep back and try to greet it
the sea flinches from my hand.
I was treacherous
in my abandonment.
All the poets were falling
in love with the sea, at once, like baby turtles
and I was landlocked away.
I did and did not want to be held.
I wanted to have the wavelets reach for me.
A sandstorm dream swept through
and I left the sea to people
who were more worthy of its attentions,
who didn't burn or take it
for granted, who didn't rail
against its implacable boundary,
its strict rule. And then even when the tide
recedes and all is mostly forgiven
there is an undertow of vengeance.
Each time he comes back to me I flinch
from his hand, rise up off the bed,
would drag him down into me if I could.

ANDRE BAGOO

This Is a Gift for Someone Who Will Not Have It

It is the jet puppy I have not seen before now
Whose name I do not know
Whose owner I do not know
Whose lover I do not know
Which walked the streets when
You dropped me home
Which you have just praised
Appraised described as a sausage
And asked if you could steal

This gift is for one who will not have it
From someone who will not give it
For someone who was not given to take it
Because to receive it is to give it
The promised endless barter

LISA LUXX

i was sleeping while she was letting him inside

i dream of mum crying
at the dinner table   while my sister watches
Snapchat   a mound of salt where i usually sit
i dream of Leila pregnant by a man named Steve
or Tony   not me   i bump into them in Ashrafieh
him grunting   me panting   her glowing
i dream of a high school boy   who tried to plug
his stretched earlobe with a huge fake diamond stud
after his mum said emo wasn't man enough
after scooter license hand-job in the top field i told
him *sure diamond studs are super manly*
i dream i'm sleeping   i dream of
loving her so good   that when i am within her
fallen flowerheads rise   my blue sky   leaving
her pregnant with our child

AMAAN HYDER

In terms of cottaging

Your friend took his lunch,
sandwiches,
down to the public toilets.
That's gross, I said. But then I said
I wasn't coming over
because I had a throat infection.
At school F and I played a game
where F would stand on a toilet
and I would guess which stall he was in.
P copied the Eternal album for me.
He asked me, Don't you love
'Don't Make Me Wait'?
At home a tap was opened
downstairs. My parents argued.
They should not have been married
but were. It was arranged.
It was better to cut to the chase
and work at a relationship.
I imagined what might have been for them.
Briefly, in a toilet. Young, flush
and done with each other.
No hello goodbye. Not even sandwiches.
Just the life of a fuck
or the fuck of one's life,
bracketed by cubicle walls,
by the chorus of urinals
open-mouthed and unsurprised.

KARLIS VERDINŠ

Slugs

– how softly you crawl across a honey-hued brittlegill

put your head down
       and stretch out your tail:
I will put my head on your tail
       I will crawl across a rose-coloured brittlegill
              and stretch out my tail –
– he will put his head on my tail
       he will crawl across a flaming-red brittlegill
              he will stretch out his tail and touch you –
you will press close to his tail
       hiding underneath a wine-brown brittlegill –
              I will touch you
– I will sit down on your tail
       I will touch him and crawl
              under a blood-red brittlegill –
he will press close to me
       and collapse over a pock-marked brittlegill –
              you will coil your tail around him

– we will fall asleep
       on a frost-covered brittlegill
              in a huge cauldron –
tails pressed together, brittlegills will boil in the rain

Translated by Ieva Lešinska

THOM GUNN

Nights with the Speed Bros.

Lovers, not brothers, whatever they might say
That brilliant first night, being equally blond,
Equally catlike as they reached beyond
The tropes of dalliance to the meat of play.

What I still keep from our long lamp-lit climb
Through gallant and uncertain fantasy
Are the marginal gaps a window granted me,
When I removed myself from time to time.

I gazed at moonrise over the wide streets,
A movie letting out, a crowd's dilations,
Bars, clocks, the moon ironic at her stations:
By these the window paragraphed our feats.

Then dawn developed in the room, but old.
. . . I thought (unmitigated restlessness
Clawing its itch): 'I gave up sleep for this?'
Dead leaves replaced the secret life of gold.

DAVID TAIT

End Credits

As for beauty: I think I've experienced
that moment in life that will flash
before me at the end. He was on top
and his eyes were shut, his mouth open
as if he were swimming: a child again,
his hair floating around him like seaweed.

Earlier that night we'd watched a movie
where the newly dead arrived in purgatory
to direct a short film of their happiest memory.
It was about coming to terms; and afterwards
we'd had a fight and made up and had another fight
as the credits rolled and we tore off our clothes
and love spooled before us. And we were cameras.

CAROLINE BIRD

Spat

'It's me or the dog', she laughed,
Though by 'dog', she meant 'void',
And by 'laughed' I mean 'sobbed'
And by 'me' she meant 'us'
And by 'she' I mean 'you'
And by 'or' she meant 'and'.
'It's us and the void', you sobbed.

JACKIE KAY

Late Love

How they strut about, people in love,
how tall they grow, pleased with themselves,
their hair, glossy, their skin shining.
They don't remember who they have been.

How filmic they are just for this time.
How important they've become – secret, above
the order of things, the dreary mundane.
Every church bell ringing, a fresh sign.

How dull the lot that are not in love.
Their clothes shabby, their skin lustreless;
how clueless they are, hair a mess; how they trudge
up and down streets in the rain,

remembering one kiss in a dark alley,
a touch in a changing-room, if lucky, a lovely wait
for the phone to ring, maybe, baby.
The past with its rush of velvet, its secret hush

already miles away, dimming now, in the late day.

CAROL ANN DUFFY

Prayer

Some days, although we cannot pray, a prayer
utters itself. So, a woman will lift
her head from the sieve of her hands and stare
at the minims sung by a tree, a sudden gift.

Some nights, although we are faithless, the truth
enters our hearts, that small familiar pain;
then a man will stand stock-still, hearing his youth
in the distant Latin chanting of a train.

Pray for us now. Grade 1 piano scales
console the lodger looking out across
a Midlands town. Then dusk, and someone calls
a child's name as though they named their loss.

Darkness outside. Inside, the radio's prayer –
Rockall. Malin. Dogger. Finisterre.

QUEER LANDSCAPES

LORD ALFRED DOUGLAS

Two Loves

I dreamed I stood upon a little hill,
And at my feet there lay a ground, that seemed
Like a waste garden, flowering at its will
With buds and blossoms. There were pools that dreamed
Black and unruffled; there were white lilies
A few, and crocuses, and violets
Purple or pale, snake-like fritillaries
Scarce seen for the rank grass, and through green nets
Blue eyes of shy peryenche winked in the sun.
And there were curious flowers, before unknown,
Flowers that were stained with moonlight, or with shades
Of Nature's willful moods; and here a one
That had drunk in the transitory tone
Of one brief moment in a sunset; blades
Of grass that in an hundred springs had been
Slowly but exquisitely nurtured by the stars,
And watered with the scented dew long cupped
In lilies, that for rays of sun had seen
Only God's glory, for never a sunrise mars
The luminous air of Heaven. Beyond, abrupt,
A grey stone wall, o'ergrown with velvet moss
Uprose; and gazing I stood long, all mazed
To see a place so strange, so sweet, so fair.
And as I stood and marvelled, lo! across
The garden came a youth; one hand he raised
To shield him from the sun, his wind-tossed hair
Was twined with flowers, and in his hand he bore
A purple bunch of bursting grapes, his eyes
Were clear as crystal, naked all was he,

White as the snow on pathless mountains frore,
Red were his lips as red wine-spilith that dyes
A marble floor, his brow chalcedony.
And he came near me, with his lips uncurled
And kind, and caught my hand and kissed my mouth,
And gave me grapes to eat, and said, 'Sweet friend,
Come I will show thee shadows of the world
And images of life. See from the South
Comes the pale pageant that hath never an end.'
And lo! within the garden of my dream
I saw two walking on a shining plain
Of golden light. The one did joyous seem
And fair and blooming, and a sweet refrain
Came from his lips; he sang of pretty maids
And joyous love of comely girl and boy,
His eyes were bright, and 'mid the dancing blades
Of golden grass his feet did trip for joy;
And in his hand he held an ivory lute
With strings of gold that were as maidens' hair,
And sang with voice as tuneful as a flute,
And round his neck three chains of roses were.
But he that was his comrade walked aside;
He was full sad and sweet, and his large eyes
Were strange with wondrous brightness, staring wide
With gazing; and he sighed with many sighs
That moved me, and his cheeks were wan and white
Like pallid lilies, and his lips were red
Like poppies, and his hands he clenched tight,
And yet again unclenched, and his head
Was wreathed with moon-flowers pale as lips of death.
A purple robe he wore, o'erwrought in gold
With the device of a great snake, whose breath
Was fiery flame: which when I did behold
I fell a-weeping, and I cried, 'Sweet youth,
Tell me why, sad and sighing, thou dost rove

These pleasant realms? I pray thee speak me sooth
What is thy name?' He said, 'My name is Love.'
Then straight the first did turn himself to me
And cried, 'He lieth, for his name is Shame,
But I am Love, and I was wont to be
Alone in this fair garden, till he came
Unasked by night; I am true Love, I fill
The hearts of boy and girl with mutual flame.'
Then sighing, said the other, 'Have thy will,
I am the love that dare not speak its name.'

ABIGAIL PARRY

Set piece with mackerel and seal

A little bit of hush please, as we help this
gentleman from his bright doublet. To do it well,
hook one thumb into the mouth and pull
revealing the red ruff. They go so quick like that,
as if something came unfastened or let drop
its stocking and stepped out. A flutter, as of silk,
then all the pewter dulling into blues
and deeper blues and greys and indigos.
And light, which has no business with the dead,
trips off to count its costume jewels instead.

The dark is moving in the deeper dark
below the swell, and sometimes, it raises its head
or the skin-on-skull that passes for a head.
Then he blows his ballast, or just lolls, gross
doyen of this house. Shows who's boss.
And what ignites the burner in his brain
is that old flirt, the glint of sun on scale.
Good, perhaps, to be this. To be nothing
but urge and sate and swell. When all there is
to know of light is winks and promises.

Someone is fishing from the morning rocks
on a telescopic pole. With knots and nylon.
He knows there is this fractious glitterball
turning with the tide, and wants answers
to his stilted little rig of luck and will.
He wants to be all nerve, just one nerve,
running up the carbon fibre, down the line,

to where the lures twitch. To cast the spell
and then fall hopeless under it. Till all he knows
of joy looks like a bar of beaten light.

Trickier, to be this. To have this flair
for theatre. For knots and complications.
To learn, again and again, how the diva
might anyhow just flounce off in her sequins.
Not tonight, perhaps. But one day soon.
Then all the houselights dimming into blues
and deeper blues among the shadowed stalls.
And then just empty rows, and empty seats,
and nothing more and no one moving there
but the lean old usher pulling down the shutters.

JEREMY REED

Burning Brightly

Summer means poppies: splashy opiates
tangoing with a swishy breeze,

giving the big come-on in fuming silks,
rubbing their dusty eyes with black,
dresses in scarlet tatters, frizzy stems

notched with green Adam's apples, or the white
and purple opium poppies sleep
in a vision of the dead

sleepwalking in a slow cortège
arms lifted heliocentrically to the sun.

Somebody waits there in the noon,
a man in contemplation of his life
as though he stood in a mausoleum
hearing his voice go pleading for

a little respite from the cold
that's underworlded in his blood.
The sea sounds like it's slaughtering a bull
across the shingle. Feedback roars

through a haze spooking the coast.
He stands in discourse with himself,
head bowed, and hectic poppies prove

consolatory, burning bright
and fragile, like a lip trembling with love.

CAROLA LUTHER

Afterwards

get out of town, driving your car fast along the new ring road,
going west for a mile and swerving hard left at the junction,
following the diversion for a few hundred yards to the crossroads,
turning right, and right again over the bridge, before the sharp
left corner which you take swiftly, changing down a gear
as you twist between pylons to make the short cut
through the disused warehouse, heading in the direction
of the road to the sea, and here you'll pick up
the first lane you come to, which appears to turn inland
but doubles back in fact upon itself, bringing you out
several miles on between a quarry and a V-shaped spinney
of trees, and just a little further, in unkempt countryside
you can slow right down, looking for where a shadow of a track
meets the lane at a mound, and bear left here, and keep bearing
left, continuing through woods to a clump of the darkest and
most silent pines, and when it feels possible, and in the distance
you begin to think it probable that the moors will open out
on every side, bring the vehicle to a stop, anywhere
where a pool of sunlight may be found. Turn off the engine
and look at your hands. Look at the sun on your knuckles,
the folds and grooves of skin over the joints
of your fingers, the way the veins rise above the fine
hand-bones like tributaries of a dark grey river,
how two grey branches almost meet between the third finger
and the fourth, how the shadows plummet here
into the ravine between them, how going over the edge
in a small canoe would contact rock-white water
drumming through the rapids in the rolling dark
plunging in and out of the roar of the river and turning

over, and over, and over, and calming right down
in the slow shallow width of the palm,
and beginning to drift between reeds of the delta,
you'll manoeuvre later through tricky marsh islands,
and somewhere here disembark and meander
through dunes to the deep-cut valley of the heart,
and falling in a basket made of rushes
you'll bask in the sun, feeling the thrum
of the water beneath you bearing you onward
to the place where the fate line crosses, and allowing
the hollowed-out log that you now lie down in,
clothed in the swathes of your white linen clothes,
you'll follow the inexorable pull of the current
towards the slopes of the mountain of Venus,
and from the summit if you decide to climb it,
you will see the road carved at the wrist
glimmering and pale beside ancestral bracelets,
and life keeping time like the heartbeat of bird
held in, held together, by a few twig bones,
the thinnest of skins.

Philomela: Nest building

I gave up on humanity,
looked for succour in the language of birds,
in their comings and goings to a nest in the trees.

I watched how they gathered
the smallest things. How their weaving made circles.
I began to see how one stem could fit with another,

each fibre a memory in its proper place
and this damaged self learned how to build, learned
the uses of a beak. I was a creature among creatures

beginning to know the stillness of forest ways.
No judgement, no shame, and water, like a sanctuary
was always running, always knew where it was going.

I gathered birchwood branches,
like time in no particular order, from the chaos
of bark, tied each one piece by piece. It took

patience. This easing of curved bark,
this tying and retying, over and over is how
I loved myself again, reordering the tricks

of time, conjuring survival.
Some days, I was tempted to make fire, burn
everything and disappear forever, surrendering

to a stolen future. But hope was
another kind of flame. In daylight, I considered
the uses of vengeance. At night, I fell exhausted

into nightmares but my own feathered nest
was waiting each morning, just as I had left it.
Something to take hold of. Another use for my knife.

OCEAN VUONG

Reasons for Staying

October leaves coming down, as if called.

Morning fog through the wildrye beyond the train tracks.

A cigarette. A good sweater. On the sagging porch. While the family sleeps.

That I woke at all & the hawk up there thought nothing of its wings.

That I snuck onto the page while the guards were shitfaced on codeine.

That I read my books by the light of riotfire.

That my best words came farthest from myself & it's awesome.

That you can blow a man & your voice speaks through his voice.

Like Jonah through the whale.

Because a blade of brown rye, multiplied by thousands, makes a purple field.

Because this mess I made I made with love.

Because they came into my life, these ghosts, like something poured.

Because crying, believe it or not, did wonders.

Because my uncle never killed himself – but simply died, on purpose.

Because I made a promise.

That the McDonald's arch, glimpsed from the 2 am rehab window off Chestnut, was enough.

That mercy is small but the earth is smaller.

Summer rain hitting Peter's bare shoulders.

The *ptptptptptptpt* of it.

Because I stopped apologising into visibility.

Because this body is my last address.

Because right now, just before morning, when it's blood-blue & the terror incumbent.

Because the sound of bike spokes heading home at dawn was unbearable.

Because the hills keep burning in California.

Through red smoke, singing. Through the singing, a way out.

Because only music rhymes with music.

The words I've yet to use: timothy grass, jeffrey pine, celloing, cocksure, light-lusty, midnight-green, gentled, water-thin, lord (as verb), russet, pewter, lobotomy.

The night's worth of dust on his upper lip.

Barnjoy on the cusp of winter.

The broken piano under a bridge in Windsor that sounds like footsteps when you play it.

The Sharpied sign outside the foreclosed house:
SEEKING CAT FRIEND. PLEASE KNOCK FOR KAYLA.

The train whistle heard through an opened window after a nightmare.

My mother, standing at the mirror, putting on blush before heading to chemo.

Sleeping in the back seat, leaving the town that broke me, whole.

Early snow falling from a clear, blushed sky.

As if called.

SEÁN HEWITT

Adoration

St Stephen's Day: home unsettled,
a rupture, and here the ruched
branch has turned itself outwards,

its soft bright innards held up
along the path. At first, a golden
lobe on the oak, leaking

in the mist – fungus, 'yellow
tremble', translucent and half-aglow
with its own light; then more

appearing as I walk. A strange thing
being birthed alone out here
on the edges of the town,

the slow year becoming flesh
in amniotic colour; its soft fruit
hung along the corridor of gorse,

and all the while a constant
systole and diastole in the fog
as though the whole wrecked world

were a heart, beating. I stand here
for a while, staring at this half-born
life oozing in the cold, come unstuck,

brought out too soon. Weeks ago,
in the concrete, sub-zero of Berlin,
we huddled on the scrubland

by Ostbahnhof, watched the sun dip,
the light shifting blue, all the streets sinking.
Then, a reprieve: into the club,

its vaulted columns, the steel bars
and long-stemmed lilies, and the heat
scouring our skin. The building

was organ-warm, pulsing:
inside, long passages of people,
deep sound rippling outwards

and somewhere near the core
a room of masks, apparatus of leather,
a censer of white menthol swung

and resting at eye-level.
In the cubicle, a white pill held up,
broken – the heart fluttering,

and then the music, a congregation
undoing their bodies over
and over into beaming shapes.

We found a hidden place, turned
ourselves outwards in the humid cell –
bloom and spirit unspooling.

Back here on the heath, running
last summer until our faces
burned, we stopped for breath

in the gorse-tunnel – how eerie
it was at dusk, some dimension
we'd slipped into by chance.

I sprinted off into the dark
and you bolted to catch me,
held a blackberry to my mouth –

the sudden tang of it – plucked
too soon. My body winced
and smarted into colour, the day

distilled then taken gloriously
inside – host of the world –
and then a kiss – something

soft and secret and unseen. I know
I would kneel to you – blood, yes,
spine, lips. Leave me always

in these waste spaces, where
my head is tilted up to God
and I am a wild thing, glowing.

IAN HUMPHREYS

touch-me-not

this flower
doesn't belong
on the canal
hiding
in an airless tunnel
where no-one goes
before dark
rooted
to a thin layer
of dirt
head bowed
butter bloom
an open mouth
that faint smell
of sherbet
when someone
passes
it brushes
a thigh
springs back
against the wall
careful
just one touch
triggers
a scattering
of seed
into the night

ELLA DUFFY

Shy Supper

Find me at the gate of some old house,
          knees in the mud, pulling
a mushroom as if it were a wrist
and under the earth, an arm reaching.

Here, the garden is in knots;
old green lifts   new green.

But I have found part of our supper
and it is rare. Under my thumb,
it offers a kind of blush.

JOHN McCULLOUGH

The Zigzag Path

The day connives and you think you cannot live here,
in your body, alone and rushing forward all the time

like a silty river. All you wanted was to find a home
beside the souls of white roses and hurt no one

but the light keeps shifting. An invisible broom
keeps flicking you out from cover. You roll up

at each destination with someone else's face, as wrong
as the beech tree in Preston Park hung with trainers,

its museum of tongues. The day connives, but this dirt
is proof of trying. The chalk path you never longed for

zigzags through bluebells no one asked to throng.
In the park, a robin has built its nest inside a Reebok,

the shoe's throat packed with moss and a crooked
whisper of grass that says *I can, I can, I can.*

HARRY JOSEPHINE GILES

May a transsexual hear a bird?

May a transsexual hear a bird?
When I, a transsexual, hear a bird,
I am a transsexual hearing a bird,
when you hear a bird you are
a person hearing a bird, that is,
I am specific, you are general.
When a bird sounds in a poem
it is a symbol of hearing a bird,
a symbol of a person being
in relation to nature. Only a person
may hear this. Only a person may hear
a bird and write a poem about
hearing a bird and in so doing
praise the gentle dissolution
of personhood or elsewise strive
towards the clear and questionless presence
of an unworded bird, being.
Were I to attempt such a poem again,
I would be a transsexual writing a poem
on hearing a bird—I note now
that "transsexual" is the legal
adjective for a person with
the protected characteristic of
"gender reassignment" under
the Equality Act (2010),
Section 7, which applies
to any person at any stage
of changing any aspect of sex,
and so to make a claim of work

discrimination I must both have
the socioeconomic capital
to bring such a claim and also be
a transsexual—and so be unable
to dissolve without first addressing
my transsexuality to the bird.
Even were I to fail to sound
out my transsexuality, it would
remain in the title and byline, unsilent,
a framing device, regardless, and so
once again you would be hearing
a transsexual hearing a bird.
But now I am too preoccupied
with how to source testosterone—
a Class C Controlled Substance
under the Misuse of Drugs Act
(1971) carrying,
for supply, a maximum penalty
of 14 years imprisonment,
and/or a heavy fine—to give
to my friend, and how to publish a zine
detailing how to negotiate
and circumvent the Gender Identity
Clinic system, given that waiting
lists for first appointments now
range from 3 to 6 years,
without attracting the critical social
media attention that would shut down
any explicit alternative routes,
and whether the fact I have not heard
from my trans sister in over a month
means she is in severe mental
health crisis or merely working,
and whether I have the strength and love
to call her, to remember to hear

a bird. If I cannot remember to hear
a bird I cannot write a poem.
How can I not have the strength and love
to call her? Because I have not heard
enough birds. Because I am scared
of what it will mean if she does not answer.
Because I am scared of what it will mean
if she does. Because I have been working
in too many political meetings scolding
Parliamentarians to call or hear
a bird. In the morning I open the window
before the sun rises so I, a transsexual,
may hear the birds singing. If I
may hear the birds singing the sound
may lift me from myself and my
working conditions. Then the sun,
the conditions, and the working day.

FRAN LOCK

Freeborn

Into the living sea of waking dreams
                                    – John Clare, 'I Am!'

An ugly town, and the darkness sucks
the sound from the bell. I'm running the dumb
breadth of the forest; four o'clock and all is well.
This birdsong treats of tirade. The choppy dirt;
the mincing deer. It quivers once with dainty
cunning, drops a curtsey, disappears.
This world was ours, I told you that; our footfall
tends the frozen fen. You cannot shrug the creaking
we have come to. It was ours, yes, will be again.
Schubert and the shipping; headphones, the road
where the roof leans loony, boasts of itself
like a crown, and running.

You said *frets is radiant eddies*, and the dead
man, head thrown back and arms in the air
like a diva holding a high note: *Honest John*.
And we dug musk and rust and *fuck Oliver Cromwell*,
his waspy face is a bulbous nest.

How *your* face, love, slides into an open mouth,
your coppice smile, a lair. I'm running.
The sullen glut of your blue-black hair, a lesser
midnight, wrapping. I count your cuspids
and your pulse. I count your broken fingers. I count
out all the zombie bones of Levellers and Diggers.

KIT FAN

Hokkaido

It was summer in Hokkaido.
 The forest stole the wind
 and I swallowed my footsteps.
 Nobody came to the springs.
 Butt naked I sat halfway
 through my life measuring
 this, that.
In Hokkaido it was summer.
 Everything was halved or merged.
 Half-cut fingers, half-foxgloves,
 a marrowbone-cum-cabbage white.
 The cloud-light moon, split.
 I talked to nobody about
 this, that.
Hokkaido in summer it was.
 Ants were carrying a caterpillar
 home. No bird arguing.
 Nobody said missiles crossing
 so I stayed. The night trees
 stole the seas, cancelling
 this, that.

ALYCIA PIRMOHAMED

Elegy with Two Elk and A Compass

In Jasper, Alberta, I pass through the widowed poplars.
Evening hikes up its dark hems, trees begin howling their elegies,
when loosened from the thicket, two elk walk into my gaze.

Here, in the gap between needle point and destination,
there is an unkind earth that persists even as loss petals down
leaving the poplars bare. Earlier that day, I had crossed
the forest's bridges and stepped beyond its corridors.

I had longed to find the hidden trail that led to the valley of roses.

From the elk, I am expecting a lesson, as if Allah has
     approached me
in the shape of a compass built from antler and vine.
Their muscles tense. One rises into a gallop, widening the field.

Its legs seize with strength and I remain in the space left behind:
the sudden nakedness of a northern forest. I am unable to follow—
The elk, in their way, have mastered living by mastering
     letting go.
Soon it will rain, and we will all wear our haloes of mist.

MAITREYABANDHU

The First Time

I wanted this to be the first time, back
to Lodder's field beside the bending brook,

the shingled side, overhanging trees
that seemed to be so high, the blue-brick wall

I lay on in the sun – the dogs standing
ankle-deep and impatient – an iron bridge

I looked down from and watched the light
folding and unfolding rooms of water.

I wanted this to be the place I learnt
how warm your skin could be, even in winter.

QUEERING THE CITY

MARILYN HACKER

Nos. 3, 4 & 5
from *Eight Days in April*

3.

Last night we went out in our gangster suits,
but just across the street to Santerello's,
waited past nine for wine. We shone; the fellows
noticed. "You have a splendid linen coat,"
Dimitri told you as he sat us down.
(This used to be my local; now it's chic.)
A restaurant table's like a bed: we speak
the way we do calmed after love, alone
in the dark. There's a lot to get to know.
We felt bad; we felt better. Soon I was
laid back enough to drink around the bend.
You got me home, to bed, like an old friend.
I like you, Rachel, when you're scared, because
you tough it out while you're feeling it through.

4.

You tough it out while you're feeling it through:
sometimes the bed's rocked over tidal waves
that aren't our pleasures. Everyone behaves
a little strangely when they're in a new
neighborhood, language, continent, time zone.
We got here fast; your jet lag's worse than mine.
I only had Paris to leave behind.
You left your whole young history. My own
reminds me to remind you, waking shaken

with tears, dream-racked, is standard for the course.
We need accommodation that allows
each one some storage space for her dead horse.
If the title weren't already taken,
I'd call this poem "Directions to My House."

5.

I'd call this poem "Directions to My House,"
except today I'm writing it in yours,
in your paisley PJ's. The skylight pours
pale sunlight on white blankets. While I douse
my brain with coffee, you sleep on. Dream well
this time. We'll have three sets of keys apiece:
uptown, downtown, Paris on a sublease.
Teach me to drive. (Could I teach you to spell?)
I think the world's our house. I think I built
and furnished mine with space for you to move
through it, with me, alone in rooms, in love
with our work. I moved into one mansion
the morning when I touched, I saw, I felt
your face blazing above me like a sun.

DANEZ SMITH

tonight, in Oakland

i did not come here to sing you blues.
lately, i open my mouth

& out comes marigolds, yellow plums.
i came to make the sky a garden.

give me rain or give me honey, dear lord.
the sky has given us no water this year.

i ride my bike to a boy, when i get there
what we make will not be beautiful

or love at all, but it will be deserved.
i've started seeking men to wet the harvest.

come, tonight i declare we must move
instead of pray. tonight, east of here

two men, one dressed in what could be blood
& one dressed in what could be blood

before the wound, meet & mean mug
& God, tonight, let them dance! tonight

guns don't exist. tonight, the police
have turned to their God for forgiveness.

tonight, we bury nothing, we serve a God
with no need for shovels, God with a bad hip

& a brother in jail. tonight, prisons turn to tulips´
& prisoner means *one who dances in a yellow field.*

tonight, let everyone be their own lord.
let wherever two people stand be a reunion

of ancient lights. let's waste the moon's marble glow
shouting our names to the stars until we are

the stars. O, precious God! O, sweet black town!
i am drunk & i thirst. when i get to the boy

who lets me practice hunger with him
i won't give him the name of your newest ghost

i will give him my body & what he does with it
is none of my business, but i will say *look*

i made it a whole day, still, no rain
still, i am without exit wound

& he will say *tonight, i want to take you*
how the police do, unarmed & sudden.

ADAM LOWE

Vada That

Aunt nell the patter flash and gardy loo!
Bijou, she trolls, bold, on lallies
slick as stripes down the Dilly.

She minces past the brandy latch
to vada dolly dish for trade, silly
with oomph and taste to park.

She'll reef you on her vagaries –
should you be so lucky. She plans
to gam a steamer and tip the brandy,

but give her starters and she'll be happy
to give up for the harva. Mais oui,
she's got your number, duckie.

She'll cruise an omi with fabulosa bod,
regard the scotches, the thews, the rod –
charpering a carsey for the trick.

Slick, she bamboozles the ogles
of old Lilly Law. She swishes
through town, 'alf meshigener, and blows

lamors through the oxy at all
the passing trade. She'll sass a drink
of aqua da vida, wallop with vera in claw.

Nellyarda her voche's chant till the nochy
with panache becomes journo, till
the sparkle laus the munge out of guard.

But sharda she's got nada, she aches
for an affaire, and dreams of pogey
through years of nix. The game nanti works

– not for her. She prefers a head
or back slum to the meat rack. Fact is,
she'll end up in the charpering carsey

of Jennifer Justice. What is this
queer ken she's in? Give her an auntie
or a mama. The bones isn't needed just yet.

Though she's a bimbo bit of hard,
she's royal and tart. And girl, you know
vadaing her eek is always bona.

WILFRED OWEN

Shadwell Stair

I am the ghost of Shadwell Stair.
　　Along the wharves by the water-house,
　　And through the cavernous slaughter-house,
I am the shadow that walks there.

Yet I have flesh both firm and cool,
　　And eyes tumultuous as the gems
　　Of moons and lamps in the full Thames
When dusk sails wavering down the pool.

Shuddering the purple street-arc burns
　　Where I watch always; from the banks
　　Dolorously the shipping clanks
And after me a strange tide turns.

I walk till the stars of London wane
　　And dawn creeps up the Shadwell Stair.
　　But when the crowing syrens blare
I with another ghost am lain.

EDNA ST. VINCENT MILLAY

What lips my lips have kissed, and where, and why

What lips my lips have kissed, and where, and why,
I have forgotten, and what arms have lain
Under my head till morning; but the rain
Is full of ghosts tonight, that tap and sigh
Upon the glass and listen for reply,
And in my heart there stirs a quiet pain
For unremembered lads that not again
Will turn to me at midnight with a cry.

Thus in the winter stands the lonely tree,
Nor knows what birds have vanished one by one,
Yet knows its boughs more silent than before:
I cannot say what loves have come and gone,
I only know that summer sang in me
A little while, that in me sings no more.

SHIVANEE RAMLOCHAN

I See That Lilith Hath Been with Thee Again

Love,
I saw our daughter in the grocery store again.
This time, she'd discarded the old shoes,
because finally,
her hooves are coming through.

She was using her talons to tear through meat packets.

Oh, honey, I frowned.
Your mum is a vegan.
Our daughter followed me to the produce aisle, and she chewed
one carrot, sadly, to try to make me happy. It didn't take.

She could barely tame the wild things of her teeth.

We sat and talked in the trunk of my car for about
fifteen minutes afterwards. I offered to pay for her shopping.
She said,

Mother, don't bother. I'm covered. I've got it
sorted, between the furnace and the fire and
the pit of my stomach does all my flame charring anyway. I'm
set, for days.

She said, "Tell Mum don't worry. I've got a nice place. No boys.
I'm finishing up my degree and I don't dream of having fathers;
not anymore. You raised me well, you can't even tell
where the roots of my hair
used to be."

She said, "I'm sorry I didn't want the same life as you both did."
I guess that's what most mothers want to hear.

Honey, oh honey,
we did good.

Lilith sends us love and photographs of her last kill.
We made a mantelpiece of her baby antlers. We know
how to breathe now, how not to be
ungrateful. We love her; we just
don't want the same things she did.
That's all.

CHARLOTTE MEW

Rooms

I remember rooms that have had their part
  In the steady slowing down of the heart.
The room in Paris, the room at Geneva,
The little damp room with the seaweed smell,
And that ceaseless maddening sound of the tide –
  Rooms where for good or for ill – things died.

But there is the room where we two lie dead,
Though every morning we seem to wake and might just as well
          seem to sleep again
  As we shall somewhere in the other quieter, dustier bed
  Out there in the sun – in the rain.

[1929]

GOLNOOSH NOUR

Hiraeth

One silver day my father called from the north of Iran,
I could hear the sea in his voice and the sun
dangling from the ceiling of his worn villa, my skin
streaming to the source of his humid voice.
I feigned love for London, this gilded well;
I, ambivalent immigrant, always on time for visa stamps,
vomiting smiles at the police, concealing
my stress, sticking to deadlines like they are guns,
thrilled to be tolerated, the sparkling promise
of whiteness. Speaking my second language
like chewing ice: foreign words swimming,
tricky and surprising – a secret I shouted
to betray a friend, but then I recalled
I have been to many a house, alas, never a home
and I betrayed myself by confessing to my father:

I want to be where you are
melting in the Caspian under its ruthless sun
until my pale skin turns brown
and I become a real brown person who
can keep secrets and admits that she misses
the streets of her slain country.

Chantal's Room
after *Je, Tu, Il, Elle* (1974)

i.

                    mono
chromes & sugar / not
metaphors us. pro
saic slow tones, isolate
,, corress
        pond spines inert expo
                sure , wall
        -s as bare as we might be, turquoise
a remembrance / tints recoded ,
                diminish

                by her navel dines &
                curves further our queer hips, does not
                let inaction take our flesh away
                singular-us.   fuzz, you water
                    ,
                    slows thought's vault & pace
                                        . share

        arms in the room we witness
        , the work of this (again)
        small tunes we feed to each

ii.

                negations of hitch, the inert
                clearing momentary
                as despair as activity the

moving skin tau[gh]t
   to pailing rib-
            decage, the daily fabric felled between
            fractions distilled & the thought that sung the
poem of friends
            & the men they have blown for wages, we
            are against the criminal in itself—

            of alcohol & wind break cinematics
      hurl our frames up
motorways , european stairwells,
      tuned décor , demo-seismic
   of wanting on friends / fucking
      playful , write again to how we des-
            ire such fleshes shift spacing
            remembered, bodies our / throws
            daylight on woodwork smile dropping off

VERITY SPOTT

from *Coronelles – Set 2*

I brought a tongue to the meeting.
Began to backslide again.
Somewhere in the memory bank.
The motion of a celebrant.
     I threw myself in the bin.
A finger tapping the window.
    Emaciated
eldership speaking of commerce
waves beating at a ship in peril
lower the life
     raft higher and
higher here is the corn. My bonnie lies over
the stuttering storm: Weather conditions deteriorate.

      *

I'm better now, & time spreads away
across the flood. If you hate flying ant day,
we hate you. I was having flying ant day-
dreams in the flying ant day-
     care flying ant-
ibiotics to the depot, & over the millions
    of grasses, back along
the unyielding year. The drunken morning
blustered in & spoiled against the shine. Sapphqui
stares up through swinging emerald drops:
    You were singing over
me four green fields, flying ants, a fleet
of deans, the little splitting waves cut up to blood.

JUNE JORDAN

Roman Poem Number Thirteen
For Eddie

Only our hearts will argue hard
against the small lights letting in the news
and who can choose between the worst possibility
and the last
between the winners of the wars against the breathing
and the last
war everyone will lose
and who can choose between the dry gas
domination of the future
and the past
between the consequences of the killers
and the past
of all the killing? There
is no choice in these.
Your voice
breaks very close to me my love.

ALFRED CELESTINE

Freedom

The whole frame of the doorway fills with fear:
the young men emerging early for work
look back on spouses covered with fatigue;
the children have already begun
to lay aside the night and its terrors.
Afraid, very afraid, the factory lights blink on
smelling of long-contracted disappointments
and the bacon, sizzling in the pan, waits for eggs.
The morning leaves skipping down steps: alone,
everybody here repeats some routine. That's why
the two women sit down facing each other,
touching coffee cups once or twice without thinking.
Perhaps they were actually touching
each other's hands because just as I glanced
a second time through the half-opened door
nobody's there, except a deserted kitchen table
searching for something, waiting for someone. That's why
the two women hurry down the main drag, turning
slowly into a side-street – a known place, Freedom.

JOELLE TAYLOR

from *Vitrine*

i

& now that Old Compton Street
is a museum & the old bars
are shopping arcades &
the sex cinema a gift

shop & now that
pimps have blue plaques

here come the tourists
dressed as our mothers

circling dead names
cameras triggered

instagramming
our inversion

the small bang.
when my picture is taken

where is it taken to?
who will it become?

QUEERING HISTORIES

QUEERING HISTORIES

KEI MILLER

The Law Concerning Mermaids

There was once a law concerning mermaids. My friend thinks
it a wondrous thing – that the British Empire was so thorough
it had invented a law for everything. And in this law it was
decreed: were any to be found in their usual spots, showing off
like dolphins, sunbathing on rocks – they would no longer
belong to themselves. And maybe this is the problem with
empires: how they have forced us to live in a world lacking in
mermaids – mermaids who understood that they simply were,
and did not need permission to exist or to be beautiful. The
law concerning mermaids only caused mermaids to pass a law
concerning man: that they would never again cross our
boundaries of sand; never again lift their torsos up from the
surf; never again wave at sailors, salt dripping from their curls;
would never again enter our dry and stifling world.

NORMAN ERIKSON PASARIBU

Curriculum Vitae 2015

The world I lived in had a soft voice and no claws.
— Lisel Mueller

1) Three months before he was born the Romanian dictator and his wife were executed before a firing squad. To this day his mother still talks about it.

2) When he was little he fell from a tree. Ever since, his first memory of his father was himself in school uniform, squatting on the toilet. This stemmed from his first day of school—he was five and right before they set off he told his father he needed to poop.

3) The first thing he learned at school, as he watched the girls during break, was that there was a girl inside him. He believed that when he grew up his penis would expire and her breasts would sprout.

4) He didn't say much and only learned to read when he was finishing second grade. In front of a friend of his mother's, the mother of one of his friends dubbed him 'the stupid one'. His mother's friend told his mother and when he was grown up, his mother told him.

5) He was awful at making friends and spent most of his time reading or playing Nintendo and Sega. The first book he read was a book of Japanese folktales.

6) Some of the neighbours forbade their kids from playing with him and his brothers because his family was Batak and Christian.

7) He had no friends and didn't realise how sad this was.

8) His father punished him with beatings. One day he eavesdropped on his parents—his father was worried because according to him their firstborn son acted like a girl. He peered into the mirror, to the little girl inside. And he saw it was good.

9) Once his father kicked him—and sprained his ankle. His father had to take a day off work. His mother said all the trouble in their house flowed from him.

10) One Sunday morning, his father took him and his brothers to jog and play soccer on a badminton court nearby. *You banci!* his father screamed in front of everyone.

11) He accepted that he was a mistake. His first suicide attempt occurred the day before he started middle school.

12) He made it into the best high school in the city—where the government officials sent their kids. His only friend from middle school started avoiding him. The bud of loneliness blossomed into first love.

13) Not long after he graduated from college, he discovered the rest of the Batak community called him 'si banci' behind his back.

14) When he was twenty-two depression hit. One night his mind went entirely blank. His brother found him sitting in a stupor at a gas station by a mall.

15) He ran away. In a bookstore in Jakarta he discovered a book by Herta Muller. Herta wrote about Ceauşescu's Securitate. It reminded him of his mother. He read every English translation of her work and loved them all.

16) As he approached his twenty-third birthday, for some reason he felt that he was male. And he saw it wasn't bad.

17) He moved back in with his parents.

18) He went back to work and began writing again. In a novel-writing class he met you, the man who loves him.

19) To marry his mother, his father had sold a motorbike he'd been leasing from his employer. He hopes to use the royalties from his books to marry you.

20) He will grow old. You will grow old. Together you both will grow old, and be wed before the Three-Branched God— the tree-like god—and have a child named Langit. Your descendants will fill the Earth so that whenever anyone is walking alone in the dark they will hear from every window in every building on both sides of the street, voices reaching out, 'Salam!' 'Salam!' 'Salam!'

Translated by Tiffany Tsao

JO MORRIS DIXON

2004

I hadn't heard of Section 28 and how it was repealed
in November 2003 in England and Wales but I knew
that taking out the library's only copy of *Oranges Are
Not the Only Fruit* would be difficult, so I tried to read
as much of the book as I could behind *Harry Potter and
the Chamber of Secrets* till the librarian asked what I was
reading and said *do your parents know*, which made me
turn the colour of my school tie. The librarian smiled like
people do in films before the scene changes to a moody shot
of the protagonist by the sea on a stormy day contemplating
whether to swim in the tidal pool full of seaweed with no life-
guard on duty and said *you're reading a book from the Adult
Section*, at which point the babies who were normally crying
stopped and I thought about the Childline poster at school
which now had the word GAY graffitied across the boy on
the phone looking sort of sad with the number 0800 1111
printed in one of those typefaces that tried too hard to be
popular with teenagers and I thought about everything I'd
say if I called up but as the librarian asked me again to put
Oranges back on the shelf even Childline didn't comfort me
much as I realised the counsellor could be someone like her.

KAY RYAN

Carrying a Ladder

We are always
really carrying
a ladder, but it's
invisible. We
only know
something's
the matter:
something precious
crashes; easy doors
prove impassable.
Or, in the body,
there's too much
swing or off-
center gravity.
And, in the mind,
a drunken capacity,
access to out-of-range
apples. As though
one had a way to climb
out of the damage
and apology.

When the Stranger Called Me A Faggot

I did not blink

instead this time my mouth filled with
Grimsby's chip cone, wooden forks
and Aylestone Leisure Centre, rolling hills, walks to school,
my first cigarette bought off Josh Baker for 50p
and the taste of being short-changed and the taste of being told
it is fair, K-Swiss, The Old Horse, my overworked father,
uncles asking about girlfriends at Christmas, my cousin's knee,
my broken nose and the kitchen roll unable to soak up
a family's damage, funeral faces, graffiti
on the back of our livers and Churchgate, Maryland Chicken,
free entry before eleven, bottles tossed into dancing crowds,
lips greeting glass with crimson splutterings of *hallelujah*,
and fifth period French, savages born of boredom,
fighting Ashley down the science block, crowd of camera-phones
blocking us in, no way out for one
and Nickesh and Chris and Sam,
Mecca Bingo and wash brook, the boy who got snatched,
chewing gum sticking eyelashes together,
football practice and get it together lads,
my hand on his leg, shower room and eyes forward lads,
his hand in my mouth
and or what or what or what.

and my new friends said,
we haven't heard you like that before

and I said,
you haven't heard me.

SEA SHARP

Summer '07

Remember when we spent
our whole damn lives walking
barefoot down the street
to buy a couple of burritos,

spent a century eating them
and reflected on the afterlife.

You thought I would die first
because I am black and queer
and statistics factor bigotry.

As I sucked
at the guacamole
stain on my shirt,
I thought you could be right.

CLARE SHAW

Maybe somewhere

You wake with each lover you left,
morning sun and the air hung with dust.
Maybe somewhere, all the lives you could have lived
are still going on; shops, work,
a patch of garden, the usual things.
Early evenings soft with voices,
the small gestures you learned to forget.

The houses you could have lived in.
A woman takes down a pan from a high shelf
as a child you should have known
rides on your shin to a song
that would have driven you mad
if you'd heard it. Again and again.

Maybe somewhere, a world
where everything you did is still undone,
and what you broke, made right.
The night you turned into a knife to cut yourself
stays mild as a shut mouth,
the same trees speaking like water.

You miss them now,
the languages you can't remember
as you walk through these different rooms
quite breathless with regret.
You carry your heart like a stiff fish. Gutted.
And all day, you hear their faces echoing,
how they looked at you as you left.

A sudden corner to this cold house.
Its empty rooms and its silence. The unmoved air.
The voices you can't recall anymore.
In the darkness, the cruel liquid sound
of the wind and the trees.
All of them, all of them, calling you fool.

KAVEH AKBAR

Forfeiting My Mystique

It is pretty to be sweet
and full of pardon like
a flower perfuming the
hands that shred it, but
all piety leads to a single
point: the same paradise
where dead lab rats go.

If you live small you'll
be resurrected with the
small, a whole planet
of minor gods simpering
in the weeds. I don't know
anyone who would kill
anyone for me. As boys

my brother and I
would play love, me
drawing stars on
the soles of his feet,
him tickling my back.
Then we'd play harm,
him cataloging my sins

to the air, me throwing
him into furniture.
The algorithms for living
have always been
delicious and hollow,

like a beetle husk in a
spider's paw. Hafez said

fear is the cheapest room
in a house, that we ought
to live in better
conditions. I would
happily trade all my
knowing for plusher
carpet, higher ceilings.

Some nights I force
my brain to dream me
Persian by listening
to old home movies
as I fall asleep. In the
mornings I open my eyes
and spoil the séance. Am I

forfeiting my mystique?
All bodies become sicker
bodies—a kind of object
permanence, a curse bent
around our scalps resembling
grace only at the tattered
edges. It's so unsettling

to feel anything but good.
I wish I was only as cruel as
the first time I noticed
I was cruel, waving my tiny
shadow over a pond to scare
the copper minnows.
Rockabye, now I lay me

down, etcetera. The world
is what accumulates—
the mouth full of meat,
the earth full of dust.
My grandfather
taught his parrot
the ninety-nine holy

names of God. Al-Muzil:
The Humiliator. Al-Waarith:
The Heir. Once, after
my grandfather had been
dead a year, I woke
from a dream (I was a
sultan guzzling milk

from a crystal boot) with
his walking cane deep in
my mouth. I kept sucking until
I fell back asleep. Al-Muhsi:
The Numberer. There are only
two bones in the throat, and that's
if you count the clavicle. This

seems unsafe, overdelicate,
like I ought to ask for
a third. As if anyone
living would offer.
Corporeal friends are
spiritual enemies, said
Blake, probably gardening

in the nude. Today I'm trying
to scowl more, mismatch
my lingerie. Nobody

seems bothered enough.
Some saints spent their
whole childhoods biting
their teachers' hands and

sprinkling salt into spider-
webs, only to be redeemed
by a fluke shock
of grace just before
death. May I feather
into such a swan soon.
The Book of Things

Not to Touch gets longer
every day: on one
page, the handsome puppy
bred only for service. On
the next, my mother's
face. It's not even enough
to keep my hands to myself—

there's a whole chapter
about the parts of me
that could get me
into trouble. In Farsi,
we say jaya shomah khallee
when a beloved is absent
from our table—literally:

your place is empty. I don't
know why I waste my time
with the imprecision of saying
anything else, like using
a hacksaw to slice a strawberry

when I have a razor in my
pocket. A slice of straw-

berry so fresh it shudders.
One immortal soul spoils
the average for everyone,
reminds us the whole game
is rigged. This is a fact,
but barely. Which is to say
it is.

JAY BERNARD

Hiss

Going in when the firefighters left
was like standing on a black beach
with the sea suspended in the walls,
soot suds like a conglomerate of flies.

You kick the weeds and try to piece it back.
Fractured shell? A bone? Bloated antennae?
Flesh thigh spindle, gangrenous pet fish?
An eye or a tiny glaring stone? A seal's tongue?
Or the sour sinew yoking front and hind fin?
Vertebrae or fetters? Bedsheet or slave skin?

The black is coming in from the cold,
rolling up the beach walls, looking for light.

It will enter you if you stand there,
and spend the rest of its time inside you
asking *whatitwas whatitwas whatitwas*
in a vivid hiss heard only by your bones.

KEITH JARRETT

III Give Thanks
from *Emerging from Matter*

For this cluttering of torsos:
Torso of the failing man with broken nose
Torso of the slave in warrior pose
Torso of the messenger god
Torso of the river god, the winged thing,
the censored sex
the vexed, the impotent
torso of the indignant revisionist
torso of the broken taxonomist
torso with swiping fingers,
the Tindr dater,
placed in impossible positions
torso of the Brexit negotiator
in limbless limbo
Torso of the fast-fading empire
Of diminishing stature
Torso of the white marble fragility
Torso of the toxic masculinity
Caressing its hollow shoulder joints
Weeping translucent tears

JERICHO BROWN

Ganymede

A man trades his son for horses.
That's the version I prefer. I like
The safety of it, no one at fault,
Everyone rewarded. God gets
The boy. The boy becomes
Immortal. His father rides until
Grief sounds as good as the gallop
Of an animal born to carry those
Who patrol and protect our inherited
Kingdom. When we look at myth
This way, nobody bothers saying
Rape. I mean, don't you want God
To want you? Don't you dream
Of someone with wings taking you
Up? And when the master comes
For our children, he smells
Like the men who own stables
In Heaven, that far terrain
Between Promise and Apology.
No one has to convince us.
The people of my country believe
We can't be hurt if we can be bought.

RUPERT BROOKE

Fragment

I strayed about the deck, an hour, to-night
Under a cloudy moonless sky; and peeped
In at the windows, watched my friends at table,
Or playing cards, or standing in the doorway,
Or coming out into the darkness. Still
No one could see me.

                I would have thought of them
—Heedless, within a week of battle—in pity,
Pride in their strength and in the weight and firmness
And link'd beauty of bodies, and pity that
This gay machine of splendour 'ld soon be broken,
Thought little of, pashed, scattered ...

                      Only, always,
I could but see them—against the lamplight—pass
Like coloured shadows, thinner than filmy glass,
Slight bubbles, fainter than the wave's faint light,
That broke to phosphorus out in the night,
Perishing things and strange ghosts—soon to die
To other ghosts—this one, or that, or I.

NATALIE DIAZ

Postcolonial Love Poem

I've been taught bloodstones can cure a snakebite,
can stop the bleeding—most people forgot this
when the war ended. The war ended
depending on which war you mean: those we started,
before those, millennia ago and onward,
those which started me, which I lost and won—
these ever-blooming wounds.
I was built by wage. So I wage love and worse—
always another campaign to march across
a desert night for the cannon flash of your pale skin
settling in a silver lagoon of smoke at your breast.
I dismount my dark horse, bend to you there, deliver you
the hard pull of all my thirsts—
I learned *Drink* in a country of drought.
We pleasure to hurt, leave marks
the size of stones—each a cabochon polished
by our mouths. I, your lapidary, your lapidary wheel
turning—green mottled red—
the jaspers of our desires.
There are wildflowers in my desert
which take up to twenty years to bloom.
The seeds sleep like geodes beneath hot feldspar sand
until a flash flood bolts the arroyo, lifting them
in its copper current, opens them with memory—
they remember what their god whispered
into their ribs: *Wake up and ache for your life.*
Where your hands have been are diamonds
on my shoulders, down my back, thighs—
I am your culebra.

137

I am in the dirt for you.
Your hips are quartz-light and dangerous,
two rose-horned rams ascending a soft desert wash
before the November sky untethers a hundred-year flood—
the desert returned suddenly to its ancient sea.
Arise the wild heliotrope, scorpion weed,
blue phacelia which hold purple the way a throat can hold
the shape of any great hand—
Great hands is what she called mine.
The rain will eventually come, or not.
Until then, we touch our bodies like wounds—
the war never ended and somehow begins again.

QUEER FUTURES

DOROTHEA SMARTT

Shake My Future

shake my future push me past my complacency
my taken-for-granted my comfort zone
shake my future let me source the unimagined
be released from the sentence of the inevitable
take control, empower myself
past the dour predictions of the present
and change myself
shake my future challenge our 'first world's
capitalist consumerist criminal zone
of perpetual purchasing
shake my future past the edges of the known
world launch me out into the hinterlands
of the intuited imagined
beyond the droughts of apathy
and quench my thirst for something different
shake my future with alternative endings
curdle the milk of human kindness beyond
the patronizing rattle of charity cans
to preserve the poor and assuage my guilt
shake my future with a kaleidoscope of tunes
play some other melody and bliss me out
of ignorance let my mind expand with a question
and seeking the answers shake my future
shake my future shake my future
in a triangle of tangential tirades and beckon me
into a sandwich of yes we can and hope

JAY HULME

In the Future

In the future nobody will ever be scared
to walk into a bathroom, or any room. Ever.
People'll be allowed to be their own gender,
there will be no loopholes in laws,
precedents promoting hatred
allowing panic at our existence
to excuse our murders.
In the future people like me
will not be able to distinctly describe
the scent of the floor in the men's toilet
that time they were slammed into it,
and if, in the future, they could,
they'd feel able to report it,
instead of going home, showering in the dark,
and feeling lucky.
Like the one that got away.

> I could have died that day, or any day,
> and as I write these words down
> I'm painfully aware
> that someone out there might
> want to kill me for living so freely,
> and honestly, I'm watching my back.
> I'm always watching my back.
> I've forgotten what my face looks like
> but can easily describe my spine.
> The way it bends under pressure,
> the way it curves, but will not break.

AUDRE LORDE

A Litany for Survival

For those of us who live at the shoreline
standing upon the constant edges of decision
crucial and alone
for those of us who cannot indulge
the passing dreams of choice
who love in doorways coming and going
in the hours between dawns
looking inward and outward
at once before and after
seeking a now that can breed
futures
like bread in our children's mouths
so their dreams will not reflect
the death of ours;

For those of us
who were imprinted with fear
like a faint line in the center of our foreheads
learning to be afraid with our mother's milk
for by this weapon
this illusion of some safety to be found
the heavy-footed hoped to silence us
For all of us
this instant and this triumph
We were never meant to survive.

And when the sun rises we are afraid
it might not remain
when the sun sets we are afraid
it might not rise in the morning
when our stomachs are full we are afraid
of indigestion
when our stomachs are empty we are afraid
we may never eat again
when we are loved we are afraid
love will vanish
when we are alone we are afraid
love will never return
and when we speak we are afraid
our words will not be heard
nor welcomed
but when we are silent
we are still afraid

So it is better to speak
remembering
we were never meant to survive.

FATIMAH ASGHAR

I Don't Know What Will Kill Us First: The Race War or What We've Done to the Earth

so I count my hopes: the bumblebees
are making a comeback, one snug tight
in a purple flower I passed to get to you;

your favorite color is purple but Prince's
was orange & we both find this hard to believe;
today the park is green, we take grass for granted

the leaves chuckle around us; behind
your head a butterfly rests on a tree; it's been
there our whole conversation; by my old apartment

was a butterfly sanctuary where I would read
& two little girls would sit next to me; you caught
a butterfly once but didn't know what to feed it

so you trapped it in a jar & gave it to a girl
you liked. I asked if it died. you say you like
to think it lived a long life. yes, it lived a long life.

DIANA BELLESSI

Little Butterflies

I remember the dirt streets
and the sprinkler that passed
in the afternoons leaving behind
the carpet of yellow wings
that absorbed water ...
beautiful when they were so many
before the insecticides
leave only a few
yellows and oranges
flying in pairs
that remind me of yesterday
more present than the present
until tomorrow or until some
time when they return and the future
becomes the past when
I am a girl again, now
in my seventies

Translated by Leo Boix

VIKRAM SETH

From California

Sunday night in the house.
The blinds drawn, the phone dead.
The sound of the kettle, the rain.
Supper: cheese, celery, bread.

For company, old letters
In the same disjointed script.
Old love wells up again,
All that I thought had slipped

Through the sieve of long absence
Is here with me again:
The long stone walls, the green
Hillsides renewed with rain.

The way you would lick your finger
And touch your forehead, the way
You hummed a phrase from the flute
Sonatas, or turned to say,

"Larches--the only conifers
That honestly blend with Wales."
I walk with you again
Along these settled trails.

It seems I started this poem
So many years ago
I cannot follow its ending
And must begin anew.

Blame, some bitterness,
I recall there were these.
Yet what survives is Bach
And a few blackberries

Something of the "falling starlight",
In the phrase of Wang Wei,
Falls on my shadowed self.
I thank you that today

His words are open to me.
How much you have inspired
You cannot know. The end
Left much to be desired.

"There is a comfort in
The strength of love." I quote
Another favourite
You vouchsafed me. Please note

The lack of hope or faith:
Neither is justified.
I have closed out the night.
The random rain outside

Rejuvenates the parched
Foothills along the Bay.
Anaesthetised by years
I think of you today

Not with impassionedness
So much as half a smile
To see the weathered past
Still worth my present while.

ANTHONY (VAHNI) CAPILDEO

Inishbofin: I
For Rebecca Barr

A stranger bringing water to a stranger.
One unlocked house among all unlocked houses.
A line of stone along a line of clover.
Beyond a road with stone and clover edges
A looked-for line between wet sky and water
Seams non-existence: large and swift, headed out,
Disappeared in a tilting and a pouring.
How have I been so stupid and not known this?
Heaven most probably is underwater,
Sounding with ease, increasing pressure on us.
Too light for many stars. Too soon for most birds.
Crex crex: a hidden and unvarnished corncrake.
Some way ahead, Rebecca in the pink.

JANE CLARKE

When winter comes

remember what the blacksmith
knows – dim light is best

at the furnace, to see the colours
go from red to orange

to yellow, the forging heat
that tells the steel is ready

to be held in the mouth
of the tongs and it's time

to lengthen and narrow
with the ring of the hammer

on the horn of an anvil,
to bend until the forgiving metal

has found its form,
then file the burrs,

remove sharp edges,
smooth the surface,

polish with a grinding stone
and see it shine like gold.

MAUREEN DUFFY

Sub Specie

Was there no time in Eden apart from
the rising and setting of sun and moon?
No tic toc of minutes and hours breaking
the resistless flow of the day. If so
it was what we know here in each other's
arms where time stands still yet runs so fast
towards the knell of parting that we can't
stay it with kisses. Yet time will bring us
here again where there is nothing but your eyes
and mine looking love into each other
as Donne saw four hundred years ago
resting in that moment, become eternal
as we do now. Yet still warm flesh.

ROSIE GARLAND

Now that you are not-you

and have satisfied the finger-check of pulse
at throat and wrist
ear to the chest
mirror to the lips

and you're done with the settle and sigh of blood
into the body's pockets
muscles relaxing in their last outstretch
the peaked hiccup of the red line becalmed

cells are climbing the spine's rope trick
up to where the brain is dizzy with electrons
like fireflies stoppered in a jar
and dying is the slow unscrewing of the lid

to release your dashing flutter of energies
as you unravel
shoot across the universe in lovely disorganisation
going
going
never gone

CALEB PARKIN

Spiral Shell

We, the dead, in constellations of mollusc
clutter, scattered on this grainy nethersky

of sand. For some time, we've felt agreeably
empty here, in this pearlescent afterlife,

innumerable, smattered as cheap shell-suits
or storm systems. We were the houses,

not the tenants. We were mantle-built
homes, the 3-D printed caravan masses

and unhurried seabed's gastropod traffic –
ancient as ammonite in Cambrian seas,

fresh as ragged gaps in garden leaves.
We're the gathering of moments into ages.

And we spiral, like the whorls behind
tankers, helter-skelter at ocean's edges.

We are the clarion call of the conch
in a sunrise radiant as a yellow cockle.

Now we've nowhere to go, dissolve
into particulate futures, as you crunch

across us, helixes shattered by heels,
forgetting each of us is an epic.

EDWIN MORGAN

The Second Life

But does every man feel like this at forty—
I mean it's like Thomas Wolfe's New York, his
heady light, the stunning plunging canyons, beauty—
pale stars winking hazy downtown quitting-time,
and the winter moon flooding the skyscrapers, northern—
an aspiring place, glory of the bridges, foghorns
are enormous messages, a looming mastery
that lays its hands on the young man's bowels
until he feels in that air, that rising spirit
all things are possible, he rises with it
until he feels that he can never die—
Can it be like this, and is this what it means
in Glasgow now, writing as the aircraft roar
over building sites, in this warm west light
by the daffodil banks that were never so crowded and
    lavish—
green May, and the slow great blocks rising
under yellow tower cranes, concrete and glass and steel
out of a dour rubble it was and barefoot children gone—
Is it only the slow stirring, a city's renewed life
that stirs me, could it stir me so deeply
as May, but could May have stirred
what I feel of desire and strength
like an arm saluting a sun?

All January, all February the skaters
enjoyed Bingham's pond, the crisp cold evenings,
they swung and flashed among car headlights,
the drivers parked round the unlit pond

to watch them, and give them light, what laughter
and pleasure rose in the rare lulls
of the yards-away stream of wheels along Great Western
      Road!
The ice broke up, but the boats came out.
The painted boats are ready for pleasure.
The long light needs no headlamps.

Black oar cuts a glitter: it is heaven on earth.

Is it true that we come alive
not once, but many times?
We are drawn back to the image
of the seed in darkness, or the greying skin
of the snake that hides a shining one—
it will push that used-up matter off
and even the film of the eye is sloughed—
That the world may be the same, and we are not
and so the world is not the same,
the second eye is making again
this place, these waters and these towers,
they are rising again
as the eye stands up to the sun,
as the eye salutes the sun.

Many things are unspoken
in the life of a man, and with a place
there is an unspoken love also
in undercurrents, drifting, waiting its time.
A great place and its people are not renewed lightly.
The caked layers of grime
grow warm, like homely coats.
But yet they will be dislodged
and men will still be warm.
The old coats are discarded.

The old ice is loosed.
The old seeds are awake.

Slip out of darkness, it is time.

Final Curve

When you turn the corner
And you run into *yourself*
Then you know that you have turned
All the corners that are left.

Acknowledgements

A poetry anthology such as this one, fittingly, takes a community to put together.

We'd like to thank Alex Russell for his wisdom and patience, Chris Wellbelove and Emma Paterson for their continual belief in our project, as well as Carmella Lowkis and Mia Quibell-Smith for helping us spread the word.

Thanks, too, to Stephen Parker for his cover design, and to Zoe Walsh for letting us use their glorious artwork for the cover. Thanks to all the poets who responded with kindness and generosity when we asked to borrow their work for inclusion here, and to all the rights teams, publishers, assistants and accountants who made the whole process smoother than it might otherwise have been. If a book like this is a flower, then they are the root systems, working often unseen to keep everything alive and blooming.

Last but not least, thank you to you, our dear readers. We hope you will see this book as an invitation to begin – or continue – writing your story, your life, your poem. Perhaps in a decade's time, when we come to edit *100 MORE Queer Poems*, there will be one of yours inside.

Copyright Acknowledgements

edited by David Miller and Richard Leigh (Shearsman Books, 2017). Reprinted by permission of Shearsman Books and the Estate of Alfred Celestine.

'I Invite My Parents to a Dinner Party' by Chen Chen was first published in *Poem-a-Day* (poets.org) on April 19, 2018 and was reprinted in *The Best American Poetry 2019*.

'When winter comes' from *When the Tree Falls* by Jane Clarke (Bloodaxe Books, 2019) reprinted by permission of Bloodaxe Books. www.bloodaxebooks.com

'Postcolonial Love Poem' from *Postcolonial Love Poem* by Natalie Diaz (Faber & Faber, 2020; Graywolf Press, 2020), copyright © Natalie Diaz 2020. Reprinted by permission of Faber & Faber Ltd. Reprinted with the permission of The Permissions Company, LLC on behalf of Graywolf Press, graywolfpress.org

'2004' by Jo Morris Dixon was first published in the pamphlet *I told you everything* (Verve Poetry Press, 2021).

'Spent' from *Deep Lane* by Mark Doty (Jonathan Cape, 2015), copyright © Mark Doty 2015. Reprinted by permission of The Random House Group Ltd.

'Sub Specie' from *Environmental Studies* by Maureen Duffy (Enitharmon Press, 2013) reprinted by permission.

'Shy Supper' by Ella Duffy first appeared in *SPOONFEED*, Issue 2.

'Prayer' from *Collected Poems* by Carol Ann Duffy (Picador, 2015), copyright © Carol Ann Duffy. Reproduced by permission of the author c/o Rogers, Coleridge & White Ltd, 20 Powis Mews, London, W11 1JN.

'Hokkaido' by Kit Fan was first published in *Poetry* (Autumn, 2019).

'Persons Not Welcome' by Jay Gao first appeared in earlier versions in *Katabasis* (2020) and in Issue 1 of *Fruit*.

'Now that you are not-you' from *What Girls Do in the Dark* by Rosie Garland (Nine Arches Press, 2020), copyright © Rosie Garland 2020. Reprinted by permission of Nine Arches Press. www.ninearchespress.com

'May a transsexual hear a bird?' by Harry Josephine Giles was first published in the *Cambridge Literary Review*, Easter 2021.

'Let's Make a Baby with Science' by Erica Gillingham was first published in *Untitled Voices 1:1* and subsequently in *The Human Body is a Hive*.

'Hiraeth' by Golnoosh Nour also appears in *ROCKSONG* (Verve Poetry Press, 2021).

'The Whistler' from *Winter Hours: Prose, Prose Poems and Poems by Mary Oliver*, copyright © Mary Oliver 1999. Reprinted by permission of Mariner Books, an imprint of HarperCollins Publishers.

'Spiral Shell' from *This Fruiting Body* by Caleb Parkin (Nine Arches Press, 2021), copyright © Caleb Parkin 2021. Reprinted by permission of Nine Arches Press. www.ninearches.com

'Set piece with mackerel and seal' from *Jinx* by Abigail Parry (Bloodaxe Books, 2018) reprinted by permission of Bloodaxe Books. www.bloodaxebooks.com

'Curriculum Vitae' from *Sergius Seeks Bacchus* by Norman Erikson Pasaribu and translated by Tiffany Tsao (Tilted Axis Press, 2019). Copyright © Norman Erikson Pasaribu 2019 and translation copyright © Tiffany Tsao 2019. Reprinted by permission of Tilted Axis Press. All rights reserved.

'Villette' from *Comic Timing* by Holly Pester (Granta, 2021), copyright © Holly Pester 2021. Reprinted by permission of Granta Books.

'Elegy with Two Elk and A Compass' by Alycia Pirmohamed first appeared in the pamphlet *Hinge* (ignitionpress, 2020).

'Chantal's Room after *Je, Tu, Il, Elle* (1974)' by Nat Raha originally published by Adjacent Pineapple (www.adjacentpineapple.com). Reprinted by permission of the author.

'I See That Lilith Hath Been with Thee Again' from *Everyone Knows I Am a Haunting* by Shivanee Ramlochan (Peepal Tree Press, 2017) reprinted by permission.

'Burning Brightly' from the sequence 'Sainthood: Elegies for Derek Jarman' from *This Is How You Disappear* by Jeremy Reed (Enitharmon Press, 2007).

'Aubade with Half a Lemon on the Summer Solstice' by Padraig Regan was first published in *Delicious* (Lifeboat Press, 2016).

'Carrying a Ladder' from *Odd Blocks: Selected and New Poems* by Kay Ryan (Carcanet, 2011) reprinted by permission.

'Ode to a Tracksuit' from *Limbic* by Peter Scalpello (Cipher Press, 2022) reprinted by permission.

'love version of' from 'after Verlaine' from *Soho* by Richard Scott

Index of Poets

Index of Poems and First Lines

penguin.co.uk/vintage